The Super Guitar Songbook

ISBN 0-634-06737-0

7777 W. BLUEMOUND RD. P.O. BOX 13819 MILWAUKEE, WI 53213

Visit Hal Leonard Online at
www.halleonard.com

The Super Guitar Songbook

Aerials

Words and Music by Daron Malakian and Serj Tankian

Gtrs. 1, 2 & 3: Drop D tuning, down 1 step:
(low to high) C–G–C–F–A–D

Gtr. 4: DADGAD tuning, down 1 step:
(low to high) C–G–C–F–G–C

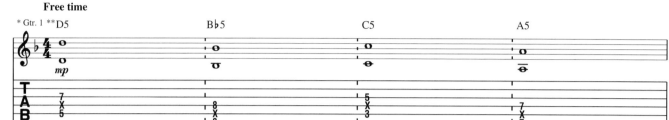

Intro
Free time

* Strings arr. for gtr. (1st notes begin over end of previous track.)

** Chord symbols reflect implied harmony.

Moderately fast ♩ = 162

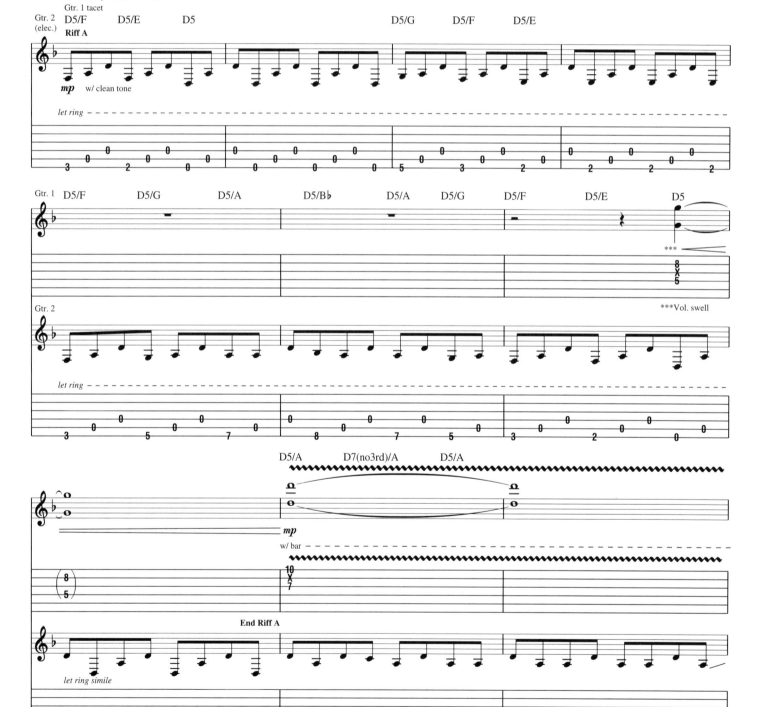

***Vol. swell

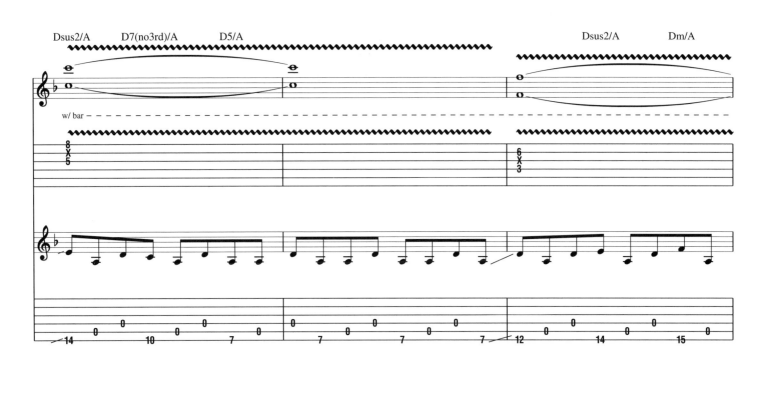

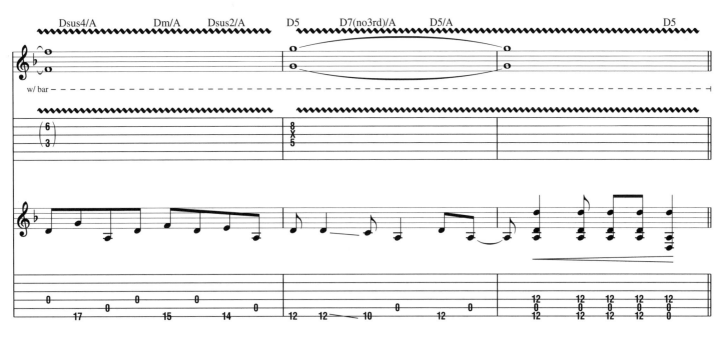

5

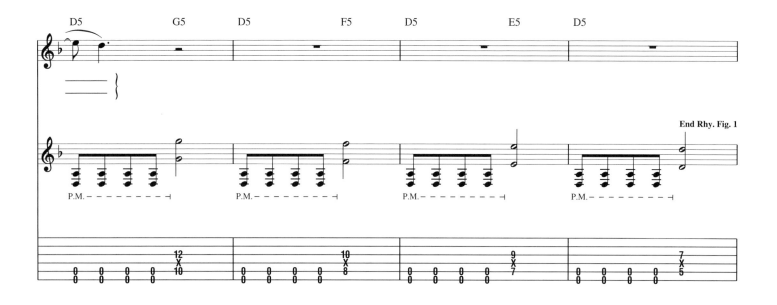

Gtr. 3: w/ Rhy. Fig. 1 (2 1/2 times)

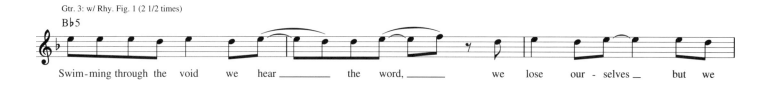

Swim-ming through the void we hear _____ the word, _____ we lose our-selves _ but we

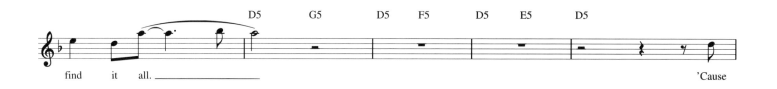

find it all. _____ 'Cause

we are the ones that wan - na play, _____ al - ways wan-na go but you

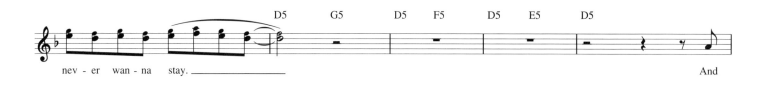

nev - er wan-na stay. _____ And

To Coda ⊕

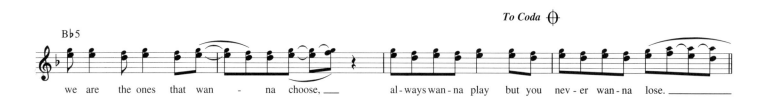

we are the ones that wan - na choose, _____ al-ways wan-na play but you nev - er wan-na lose. _____

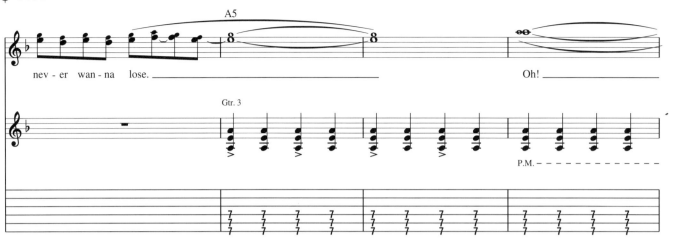

nev - er wan - na lose. _____ Oh! _____

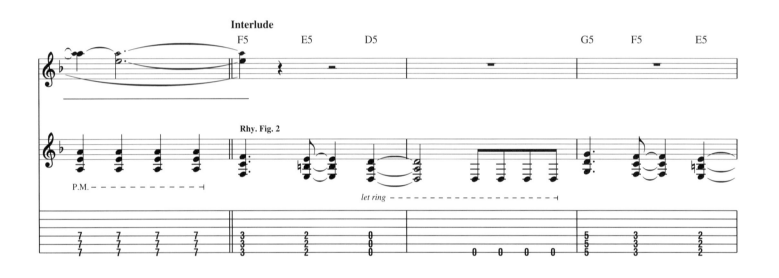

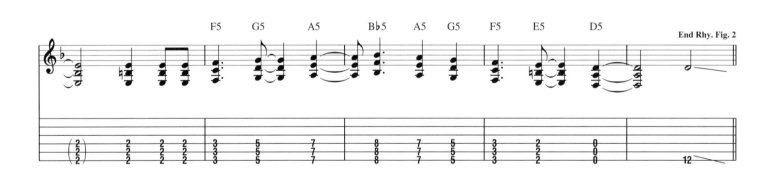

Chorus

Gtr. 3: w/ Rhy. Fig. 2 (2 times)

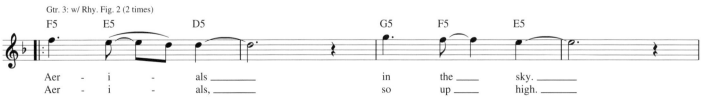

Aer - i - als _____ in the _____ sky. _____
Aer - i - als, _____ so up _____ high. _____

When you ___ lose ___ small ___ mind, you free ___ your ___ life. ___
When you ___ free ___ your ___ eyes, e - ter - nal ___ prize. ___

Chorus

Gtrs. 2 & 4: w/ Riffs A & B (2 times)

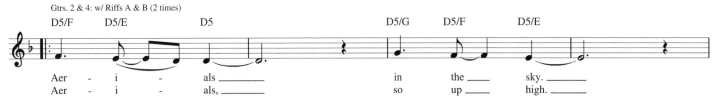

Aer - i - als ___ in the ___ sky. ___
Aer - i - als, ___ so up ___ high. ___

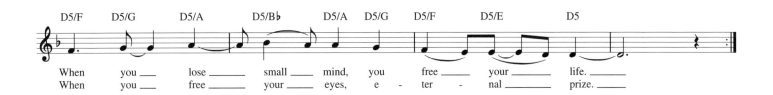

When you ___ lose ___ small ___ mind, you free ___ your ___ life. ___
When you ___ free ___ your ___ eyes, e - ter - nal ___ prize. ___

Outro

Gtrs. 2 & 4: w/ Riffs A & B (1 3/4 times)

Ah, ___ ah. ___ Ah. ___

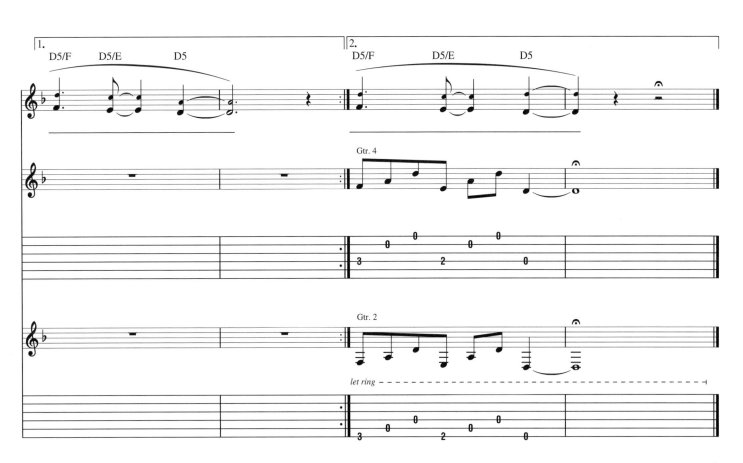

All the Small Things

Words and Music by Tom De Longe and Mark Hoppus

Verse

Gtr. 1: w/ Rhy. Fig. 2
Gtr. 2 tacet

2. Late night, come home. _____ Work sucks, I know. __

D.S. al Coda

Gtr. 1: w/ Rhy. Fig. 3

__ She left me ros - es by the stairs. _ Sur - pris - es let me know she cares. _

⊕ *Coda*

Interlude

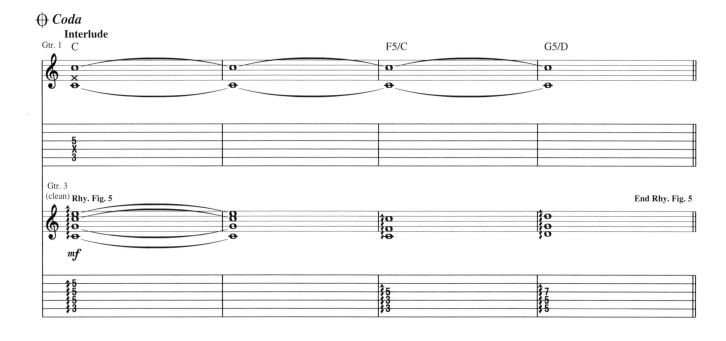

Gtr. 3: w/ Rhy. Fig. 5, 3 times

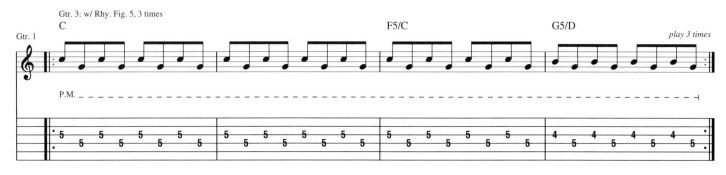

Say it ain't so. I will not __ go. Turn the lights _ off. Car - ry me __

Outro

Gtr. 1: w/ Rhy. Fig. 4, 2 times
Gtr. 2: w/ Riff A, 3 1/2 times

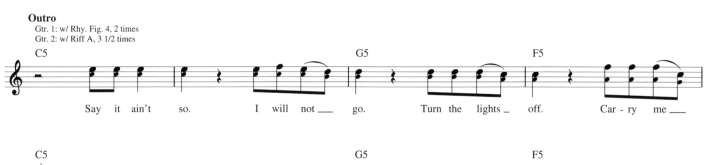

home. Keep your head still. I'll be your _ thrill. The night will go __ on, my lit - tle wind -

Behind Blue Eyes

Words and Music by Pete Townshend

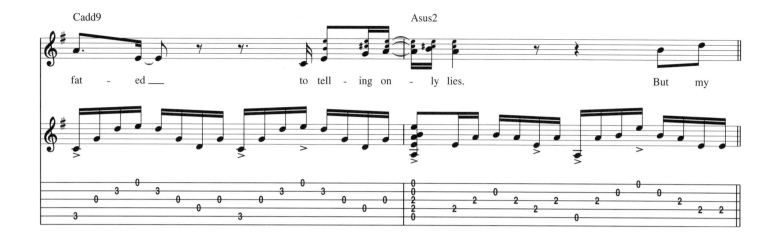

Chorus

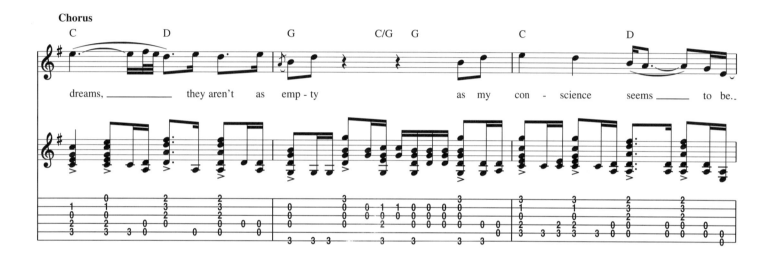

Interlude

-vil, put your fin - ger down. my throat. And if I shiv - er, please give me a

blan - ket, keep me warm, _ let me wear your coat. _

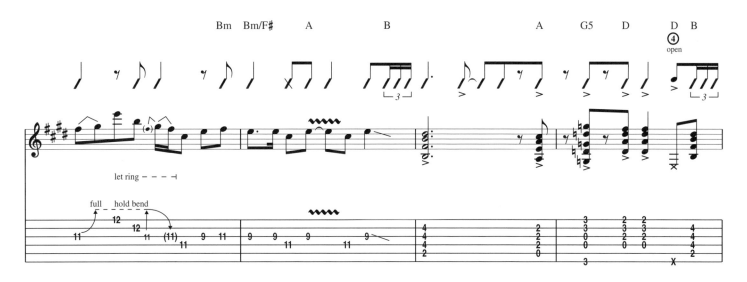

let ring - - - -

full   hold bend

* vib w/ neck

vib w/ neck

* Vibrato achieved by applying force with right hand on gtr. body & left hand on neck.

(cont. in notation)

Outro
Half-Time ♩ = 60

Gtr. 2 tacet

N - no one knows what it's like __ to be the

Gtr. 1

Gtr. 2

bad man, __ to be the sad man __ be-hind __ blue eyes. __

poco rit.

poco rit.

Cat Scratch Fever

Words and Music by Ted Nugent

It makes a grown man   cry,_____   cry._____ Oh, won't you   bite   my   fur.

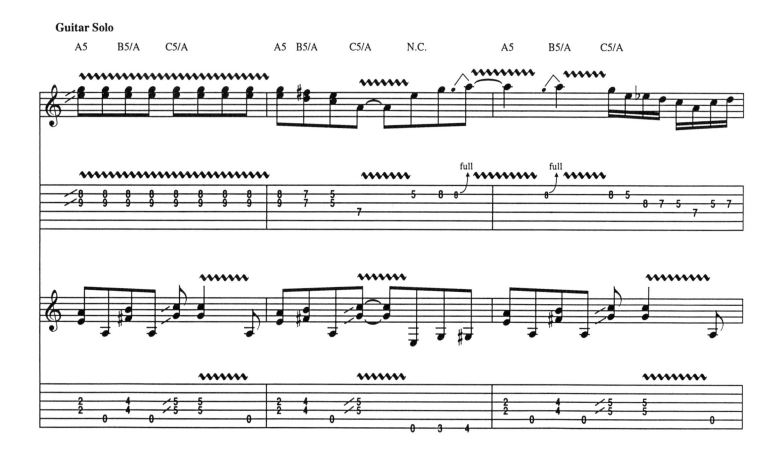

Guitar Solo

Verse

3. Well, I make___ a pus-sy purr with a stroke of my hand.___

They know they get-tin' it from me.___ And they know___ just where to go when they

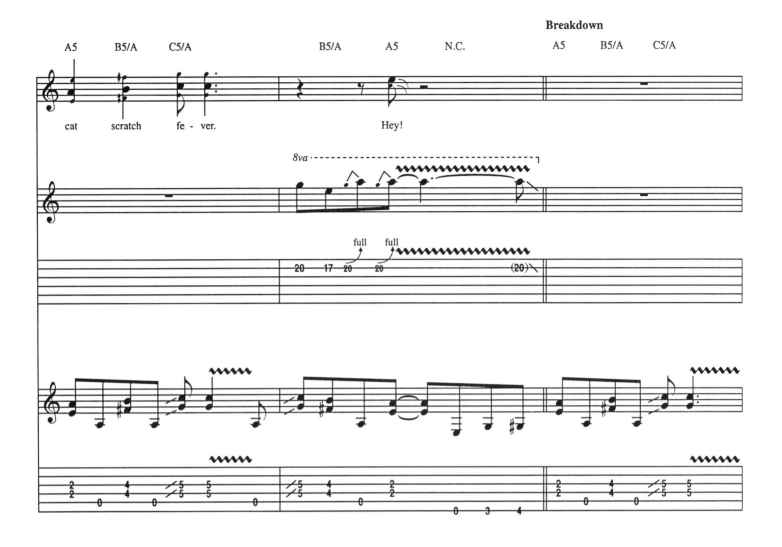

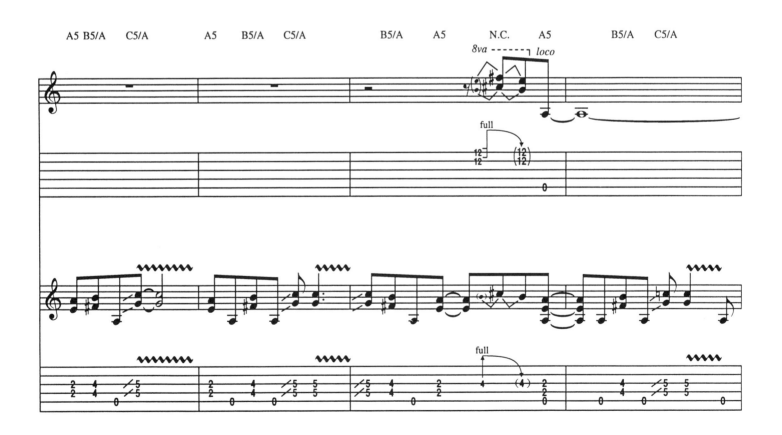

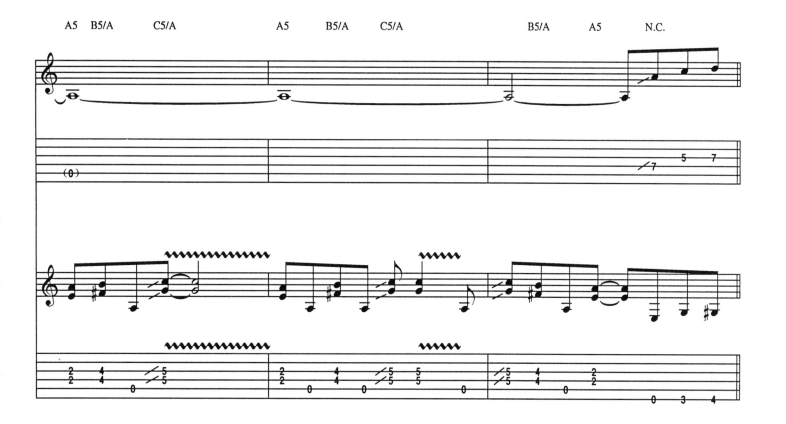

Chorus

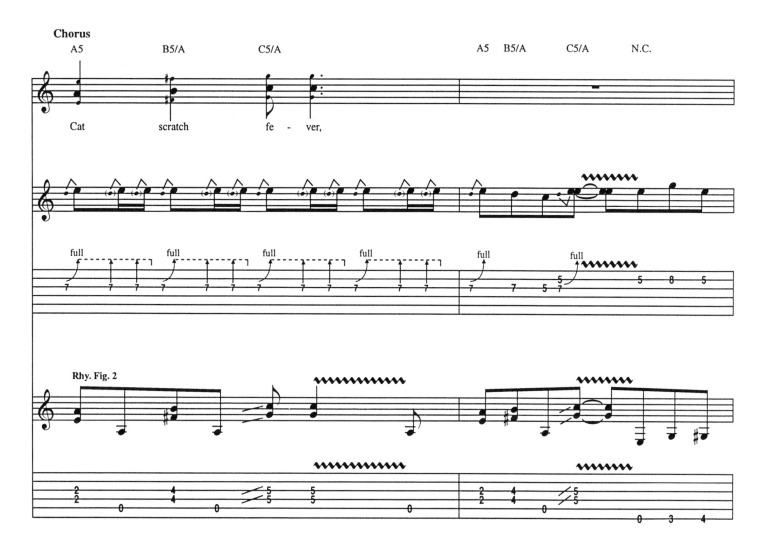

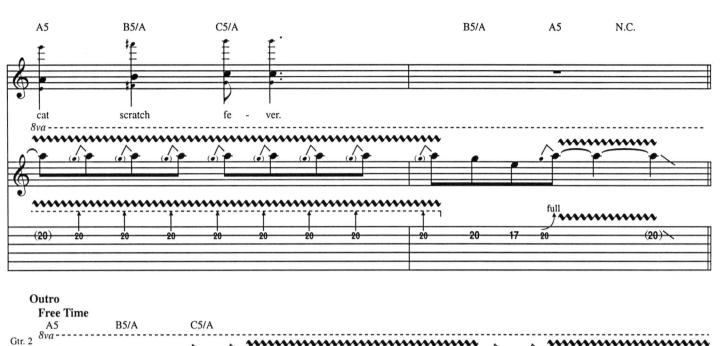

Outro
Free Time

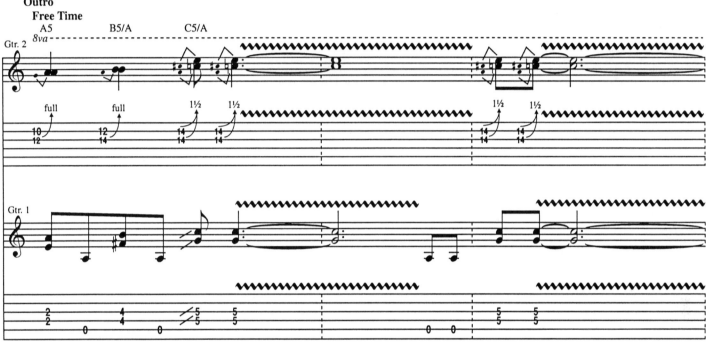

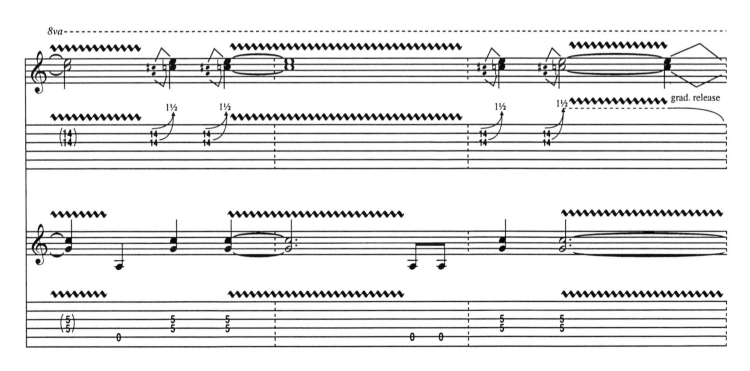

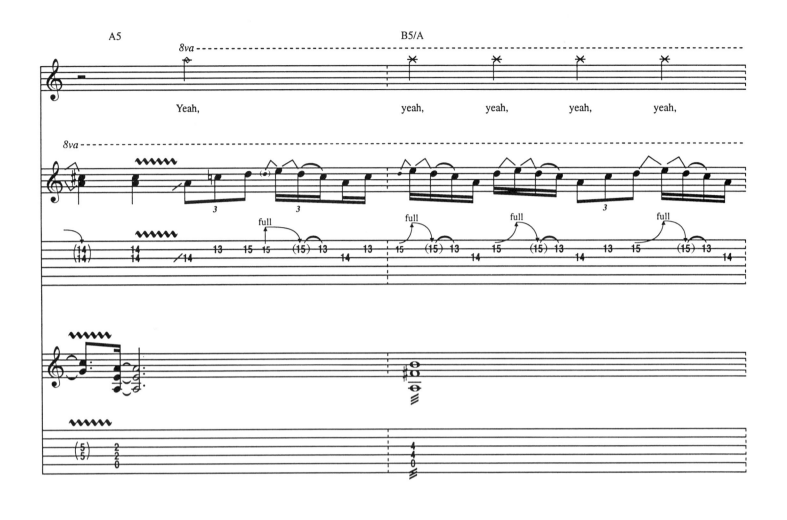

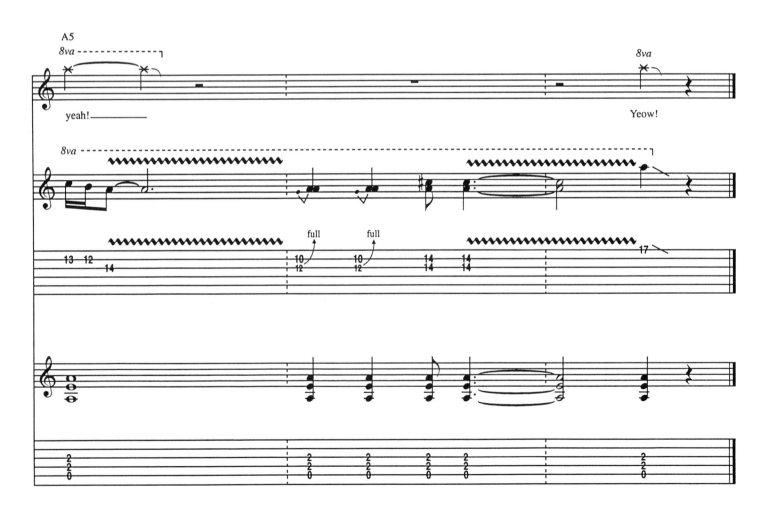

Love Me Two Times

Words and Music by The Doors

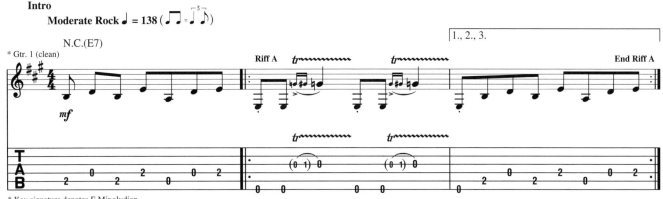

* Key signature denotes E Mixolydian.

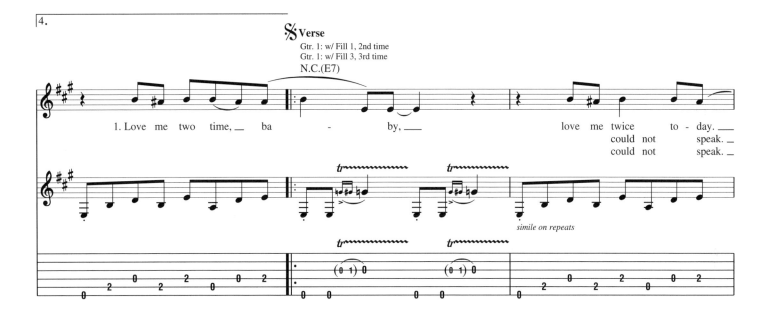

Pre-Chorus

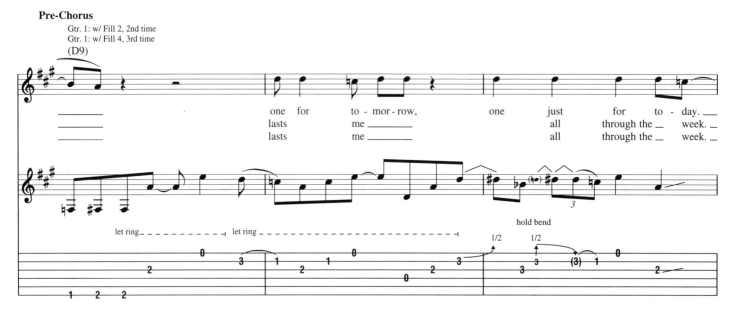

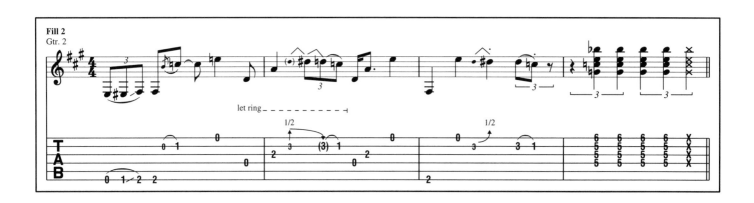

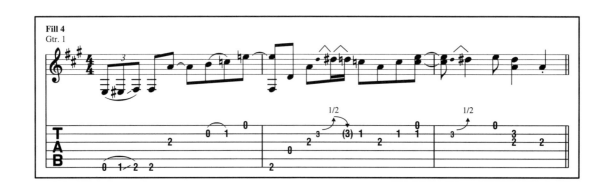

Oye Como Va

Words and Music by Tito Puente

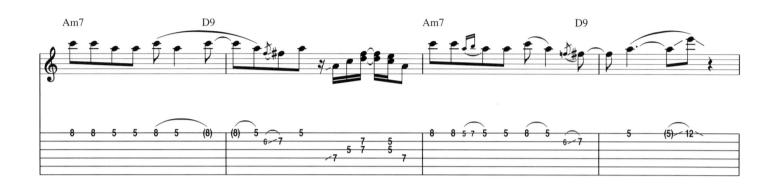

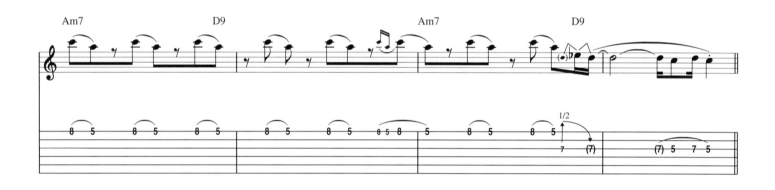

Interlude

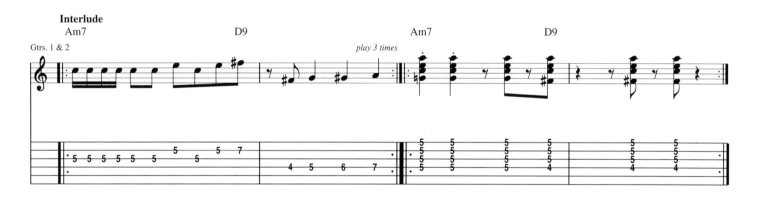

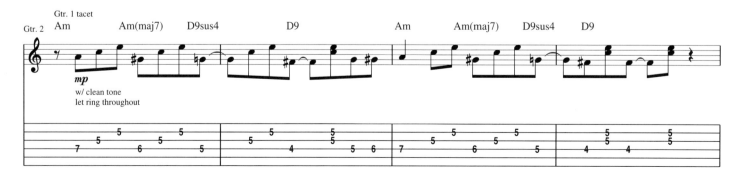

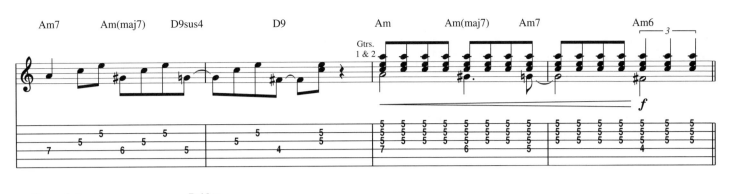

Organ Solo
Gtr. 2: w/ Rhy. Fig. 1, 11 times, simile

Bridge
Gtrs. 1 & 2: w/ Rhy. Fig. 1, 2 times

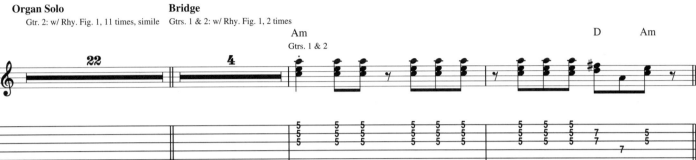

Verse
Gtrs. 1 & 2: w/ Rhy. Fig. 1, 2 times, simile

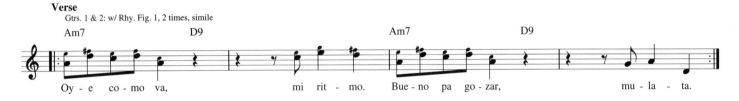

Oy - e co - mo va, mi rit - mo. Bue - no pa go - zar, mu - la - ta.

Bridge

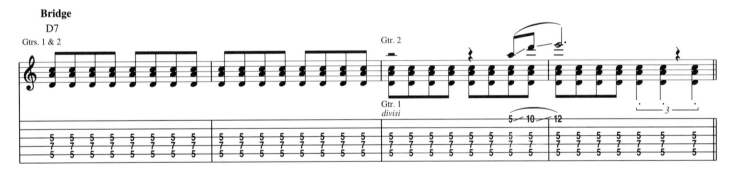

Guitar Solo
Gtr. 1: w/ Rhy. Fig. 1, 12 times, simile

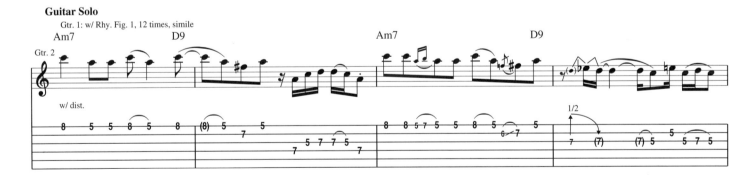

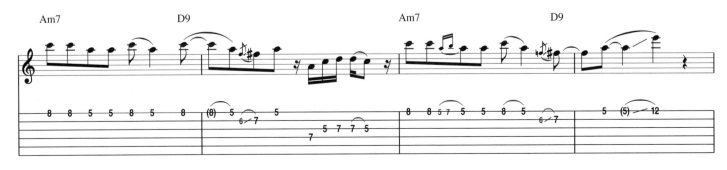

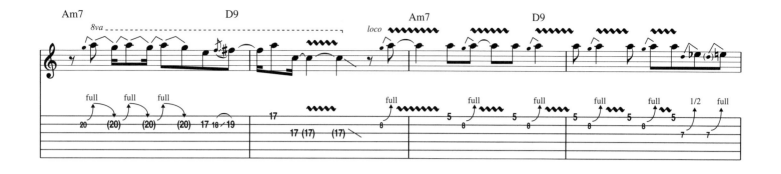

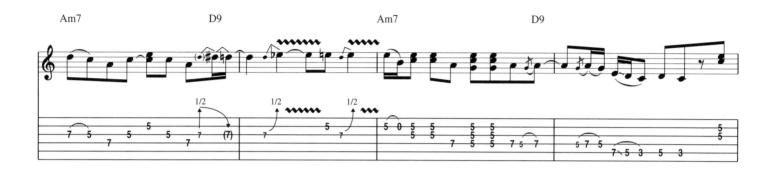

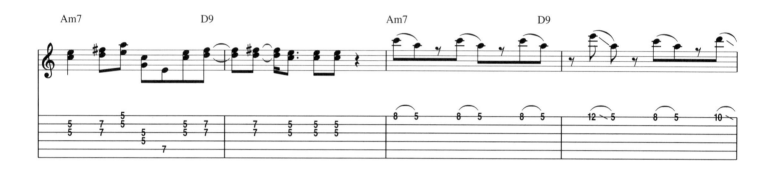

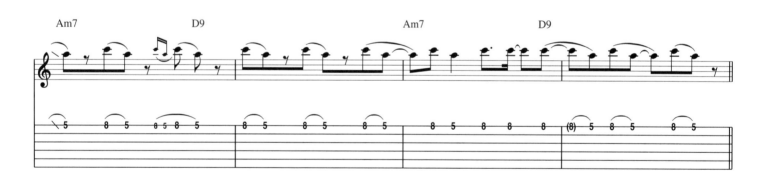

Outro

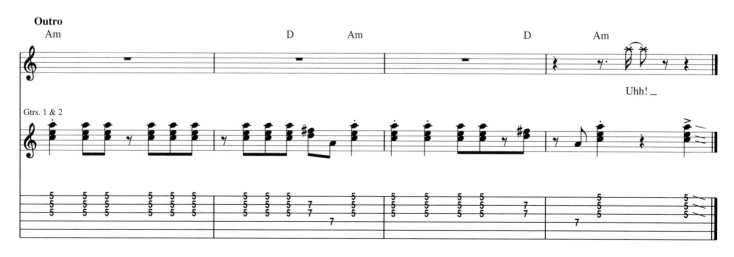

Rock and Roll Never Forgets

Words and Music by Bob Seger

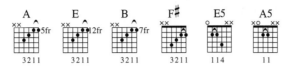

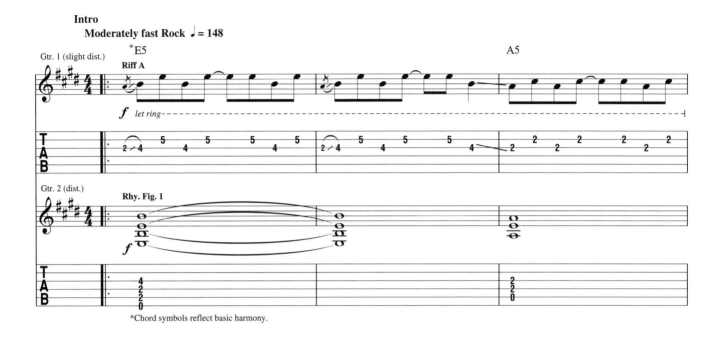

*Chord symbols reflect basic harmony.

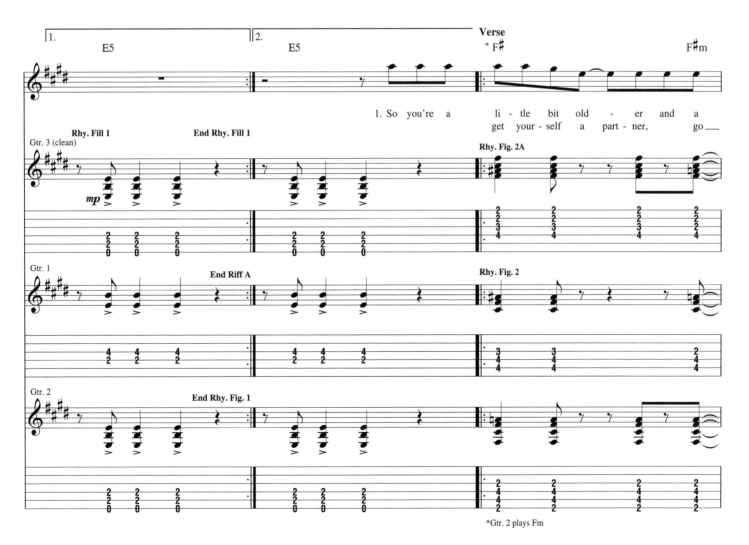

*Gtr. 2 plays Fm

dig - ni - ty. _____ So, now
_____ too far. _____ Yeah, the

End Rhy. Fig. 2A

(cont. in slashes)

End Rhy. Fig. 2

P.M.

Pre-Chorus

A   E   A

Rhy. Fig. 3

Gtr. 3

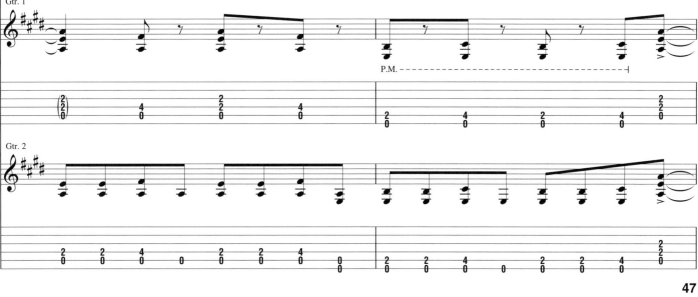

sweet six - teen's turned thir - ty - one, _____ you
raf - ters will be ring - ing 'cause the beat's so strong, _____ the
sweet six - teen's turned thir - ty - one, _____

Gtr. 1

P.M.

Gtr. 2

get to feel-in' wear-y when the work day's done._____ Well, all _____
crowd will be sway-ing and sing-ing a-long._____ And all _____
feel a lit-tle ti-red, feel-ing un-der the gun._____ Well, all _____

End Rhy. Fig. 3

_____ you got to do is get up and in-to your kicks ___
_____ you got to do is get in, in-to the mix ___
_____ of Chuck's chil-dren are out _____ there, play-ing his licks.

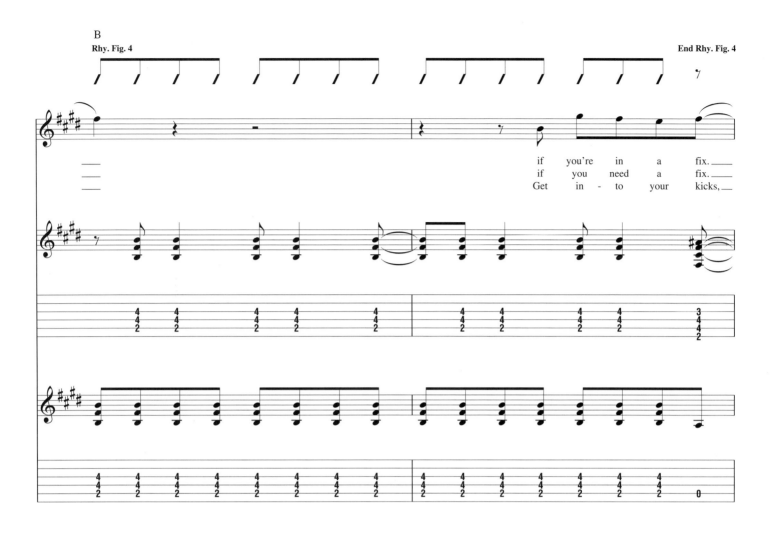

if you're in a fix. ___
if you need a fix. ___
Get in - to your kicks, ___

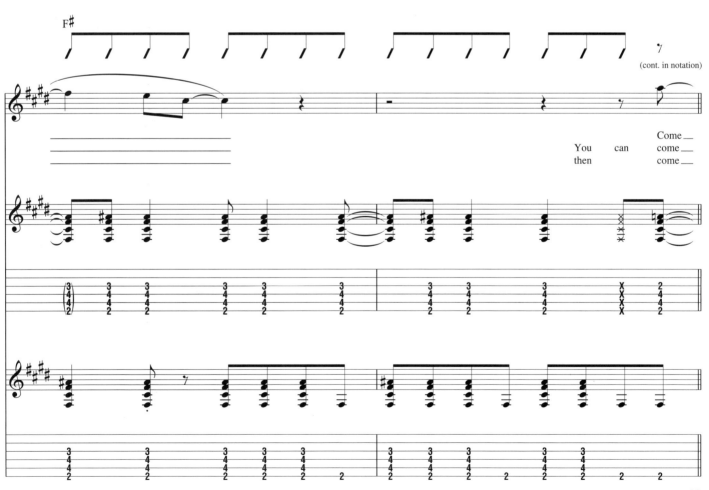

Come ___
You can come ___
then come ___

Guitar Solo

Gtrs. 1 & 3: w/ Rhy. Figs. 2 & 2A

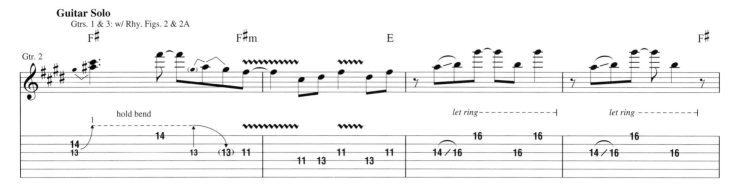

D.S. al Coda

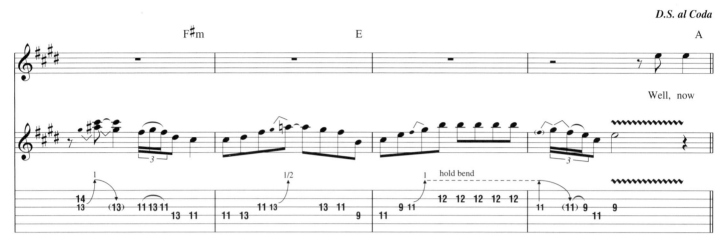

⊕ **Coda**

Gtrs. 1, 2 & 3: w/ Rhy. Figs. 5, 5A & 5B (1st 3 meas.)

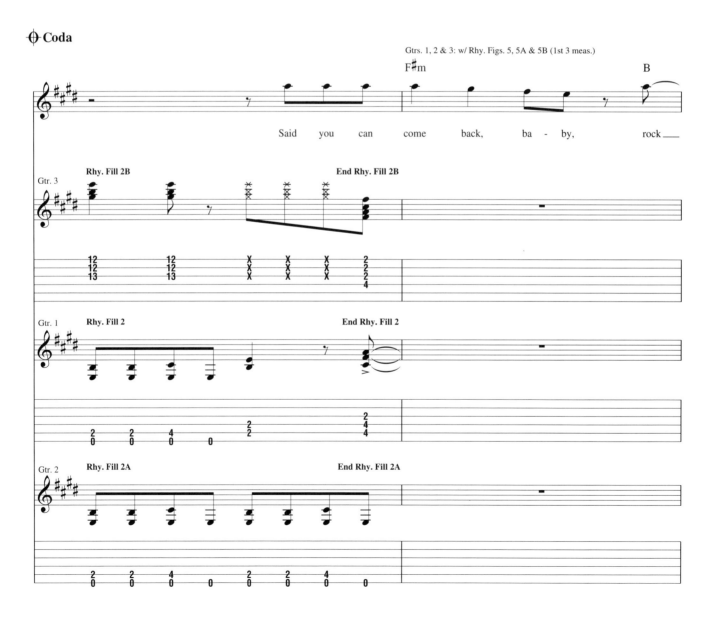

__ 'n roll nev - er for - gets. ____ Oh, come __ back, ba - by, rock

__ 'n roll nev - er for - gets. ____ Oo. _____

Interlude

Gtr. 1: w/ Riff A (2 times)
Gtr. 2: w/ Rhy. Fig. 1 (2 times)
Gtr. 3: w/ Rhy. Fill 1

_____ Oh, yeah. __ Oh, yeah. __

Gtr. 3: w/ Rhy. Fill 1

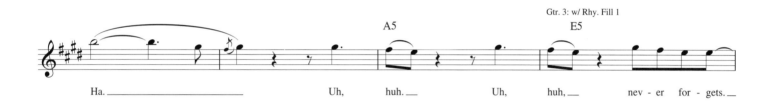

Ha. _____ Uh, huh. __ Uh, huh, __ nev - er for - gets. __

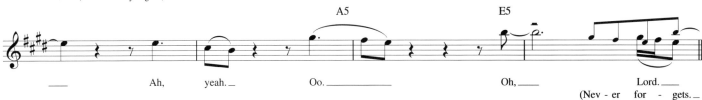

Outro-Guitar Solo

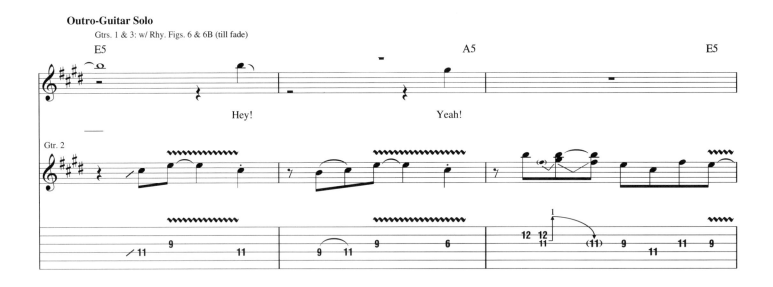

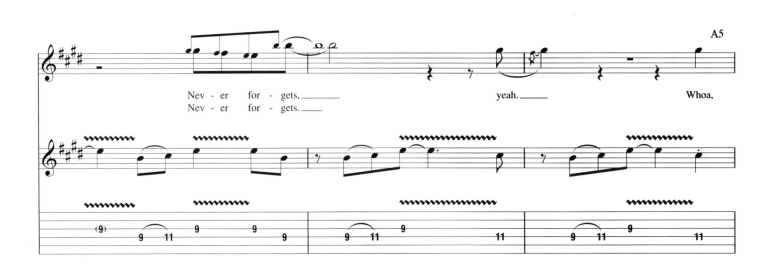

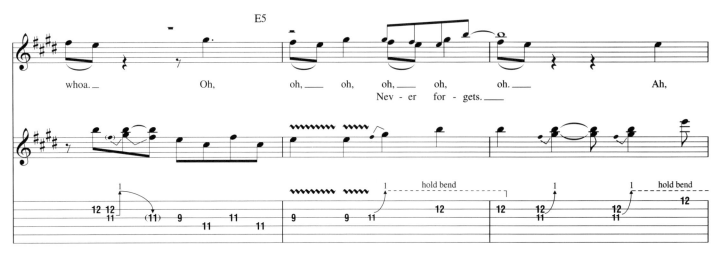

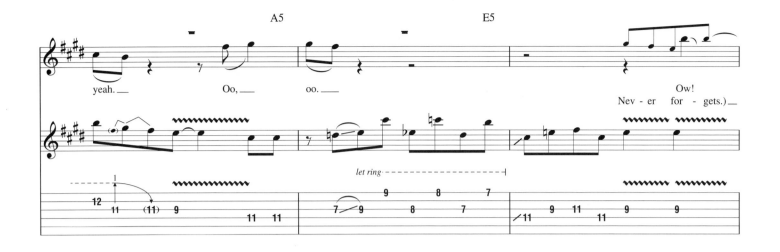

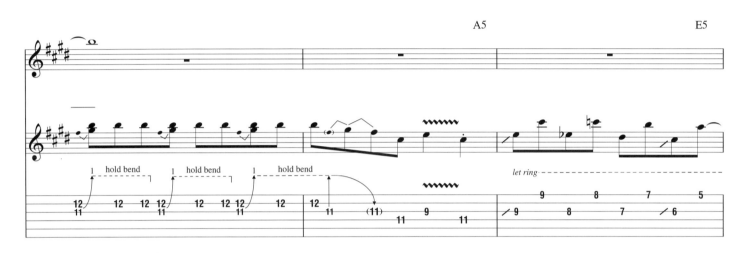

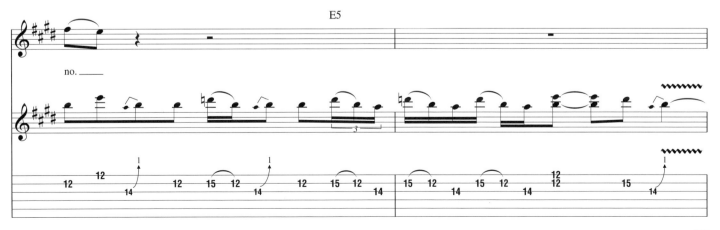

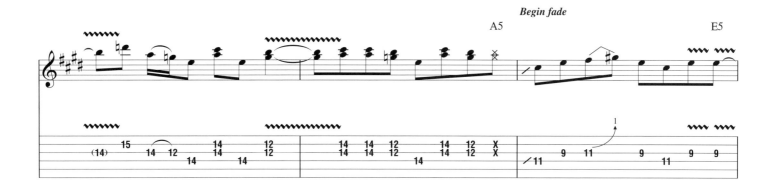

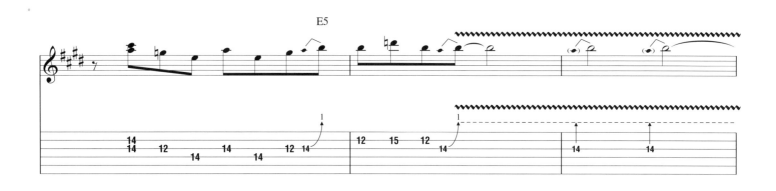

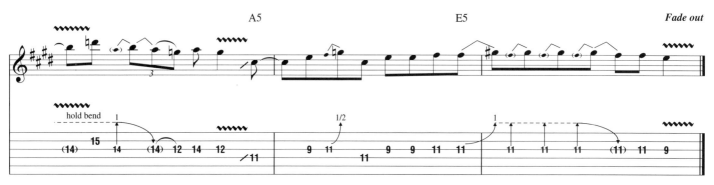

Scar Tissue

Words and Music by Anthony Kiedis, Flea, John Frusciante and Chad Smith

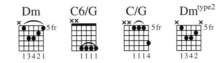

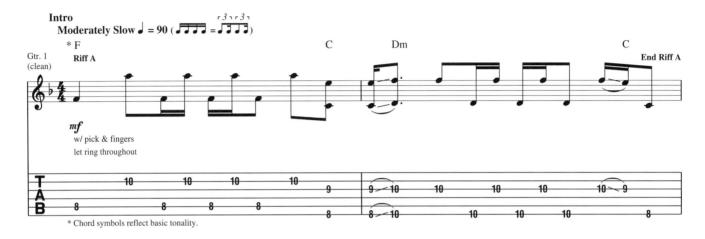

* Chord symbols reflect basic tonality.

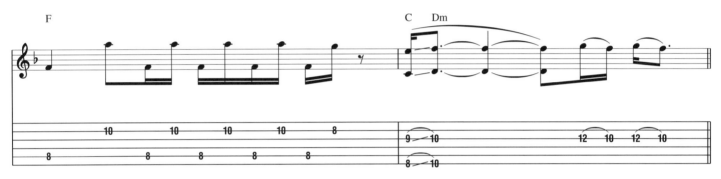

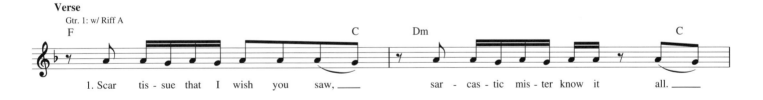

1. Scar tis-sue that I wish you saw, ___ sar-cas-tic mis-ter know it all. ___

Close your eyes and I'll ___ kiss you 'cause ___ with the birds I'll share, ___

with the birds I'll share this lone - ly view._____
Share ___ this lone - ly...)

60

Guitar Solo

Verse

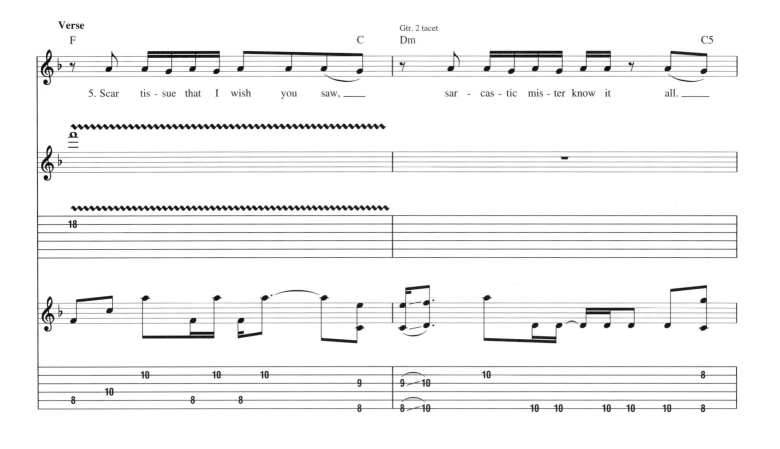

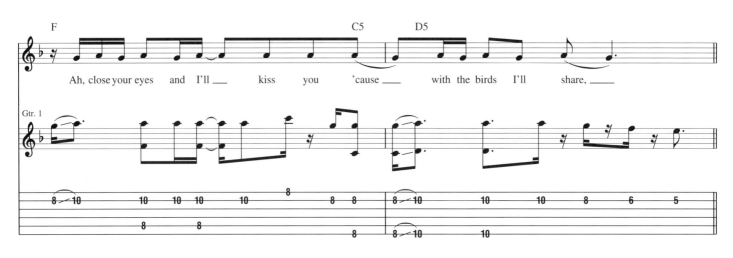

Chorus

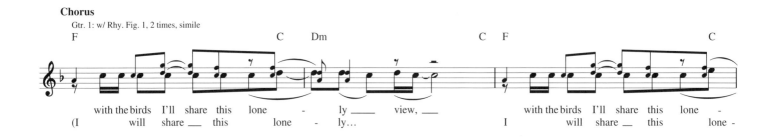

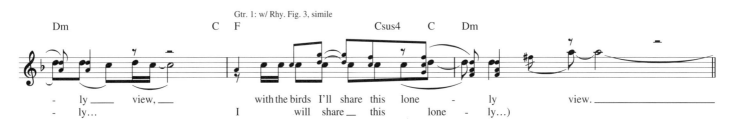

Outro-Guitar Solo

All You Need Is Love

Words and Music by John Lennon and Paul McCartney

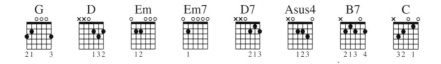

* Strum Pattern: 3, 8
* Pick Pattern: 3, 8

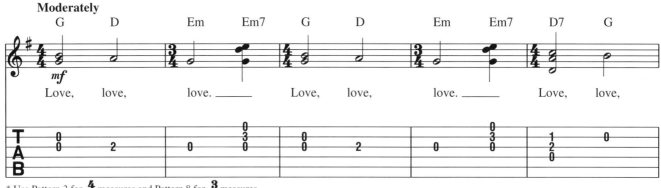

* Use Pattern 3 for 4/4 measures and Pattern 8 for 3/4 measures.

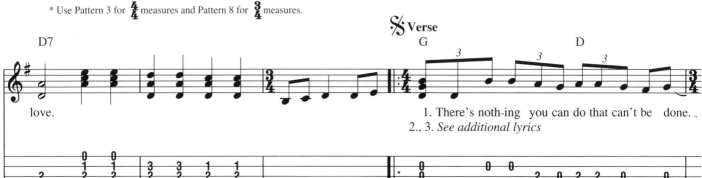

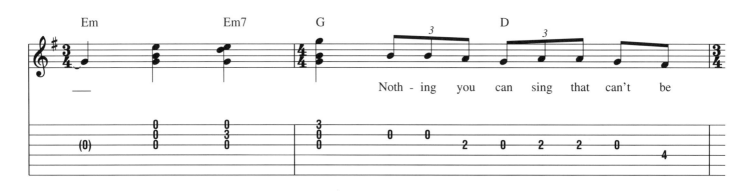

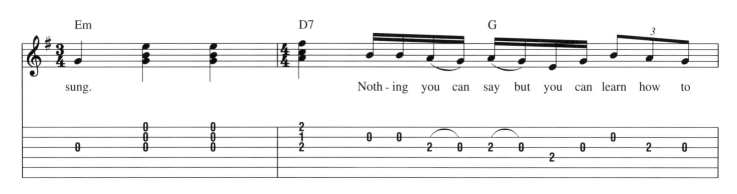

⊕ Coda

Chorus

All you need is love. ___ *Spoken: All to-geth-er now.* All you need is love. _

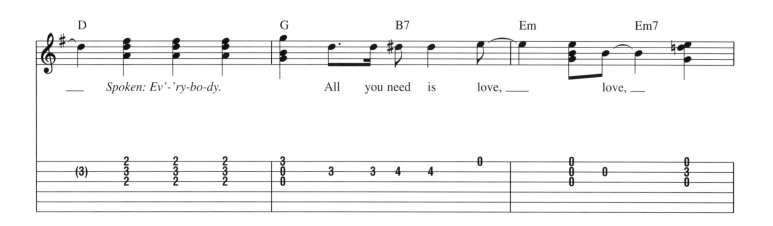

_ *Spoken: Ev'-'ry-bo-dy.* All you need is love, ___ love, ___

Repeat and fade

Outro

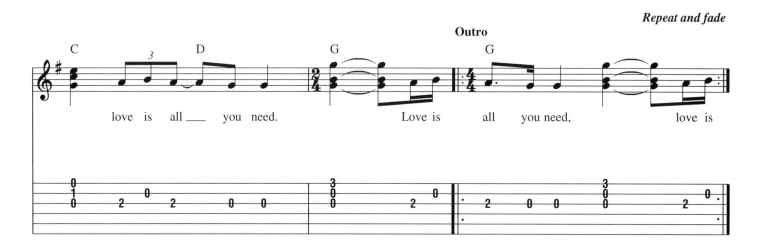

love is all ___ you need. Love is all you need, love is

Additional Lyrics

2. There's nothing you can make that can't be made.
   No one you can save that can't be saved.
   Nothing you can do but you can learn how to be you in time.
   It's easy.

3. There's nothing you can know that isn't known.
   Nothing you can see that isn't shown.
   Nowhere you can be that isn't where you're meant to be.
   It's easy.

Bluesette

Words by Norman Gimbel
Music by Jean Thielemans

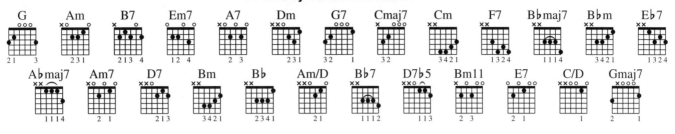

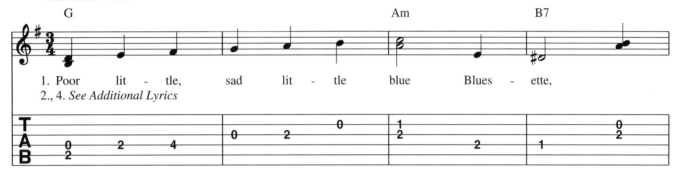

Strum Pattern: 8
Pick Pattern: 8

Verse
Moderate Waltz

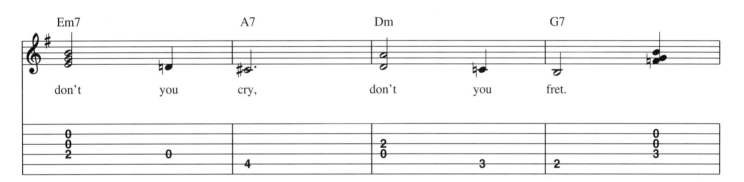

1. Poor lit - tle, sad lit - tle blue Blues - ette,
2., 4. *See Additional Lyrics*

don't you cry, don't you fret.

You can bet one luck - y day you'll 'wak - en

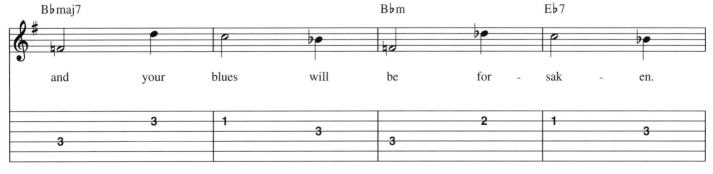

and your blues will be for - sak - en.

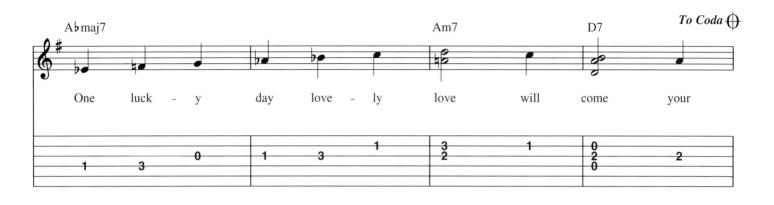

One luck - y day love - ly love will come your

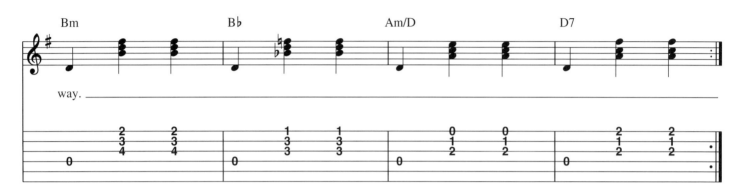

way.

Bridge

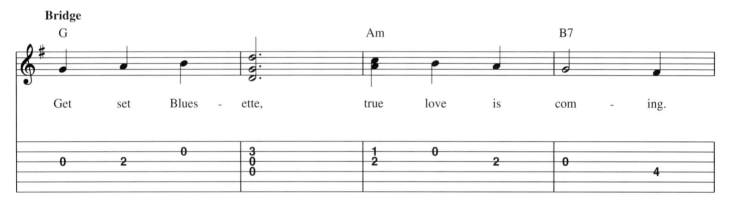

Get set Blues - ette, true love is com - ing.

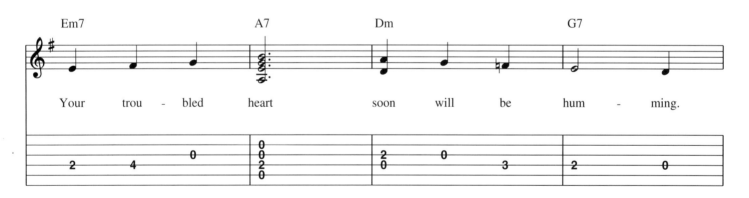

Your trou - bled heart soon will be hum - ming.

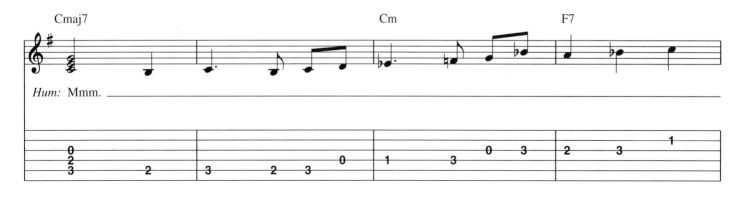

Hum: Mmm.

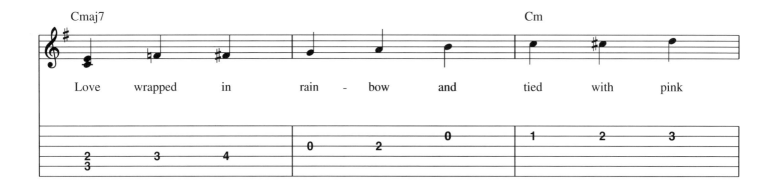

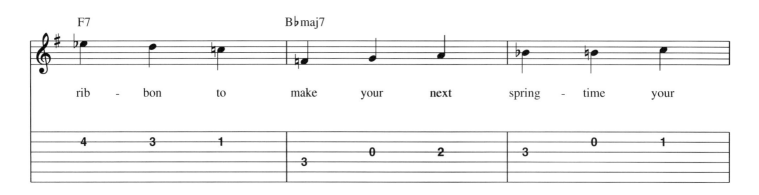

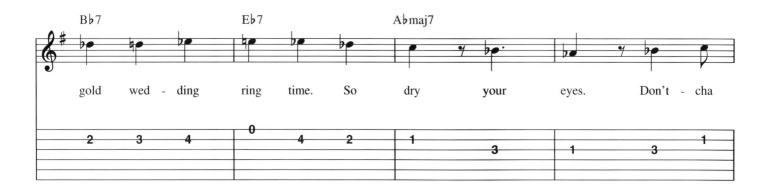

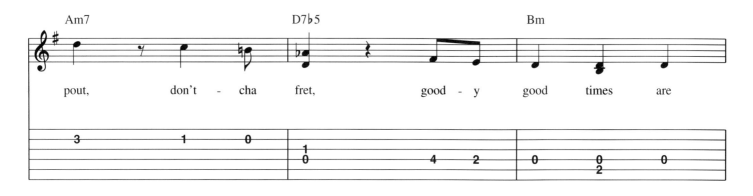

D.C. al Coda

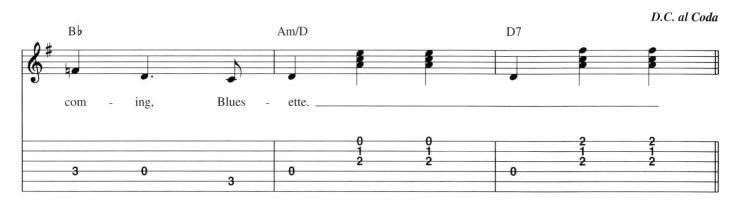

Coda

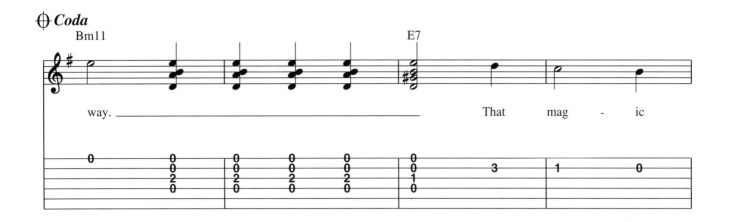

way. _____ That mag - ic

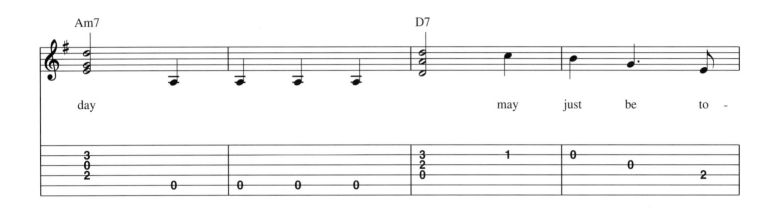

day may just be to -

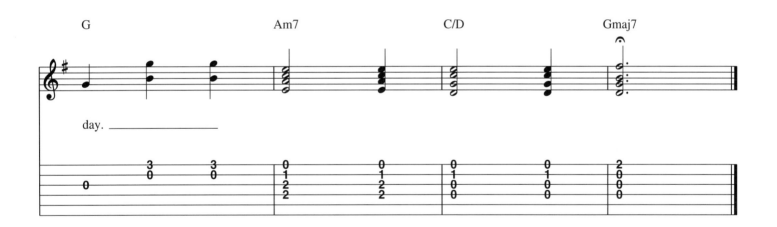

day. _____

Additional Lyrics

2. Long as there's love in your heart to share,
   Dear Bluesette, don't dispair.
   Some blue boy is longing, just like you,
   To find someone to be true to.
   Two loving arms he can nestle in and stay.

3. Long as there's love in your heart to share,
   Dear Bluesette, don't dispair.
   Some blue boy is longing, just like you,
   To find someone to be true to.
   One lucky day lovely love will come your way.

Bewitched

from PAL JOEY
Words by Lorenz Hart
Music by Richard Rodgers

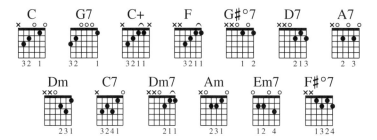

Strum Pattern: 2
Pick Pattern: 4

F   A7   Dm   Dm7

I. _____ Lost my heart, ___ but what of it?_____

Am   Dm7   G7   Dm7   G7

He is cold ___ I a - gree, _____ he can laugh, __ but I love it, _____ al-though the

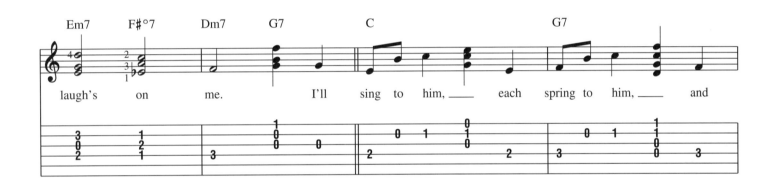

Em7   F#°7   Dm7   G7   C   G7

laugh's on me. I'll sing to him, ___ each spring to him, ___ and

C   C+   F   G#°7   C   D7   Dm   G7

long for the day when I'll cling to him. ___ Be - witched, both-ered and be - wild - ered ___ am

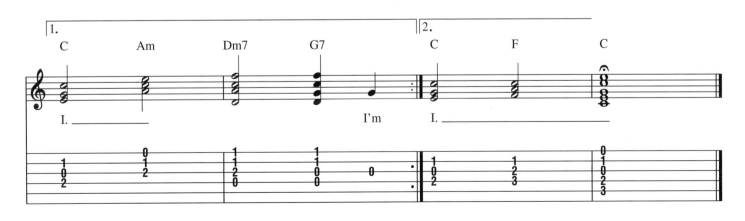

1.

C   Am   Dm7   G7   2. C   F   C

I. _____ I'm   I. _____

California Girls

Words and Music by Brian Wilson and Mike Love

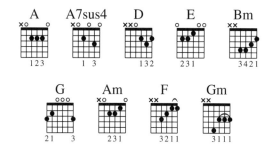

Strum Pattern: 1, 2
Pick Pattern: 2, 4

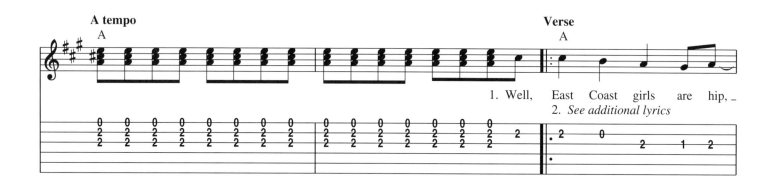

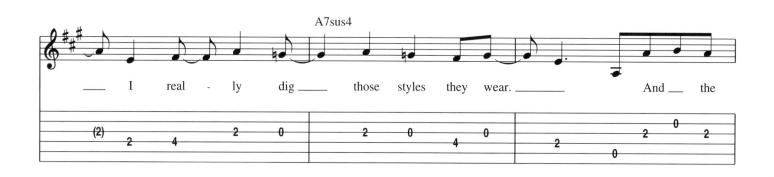

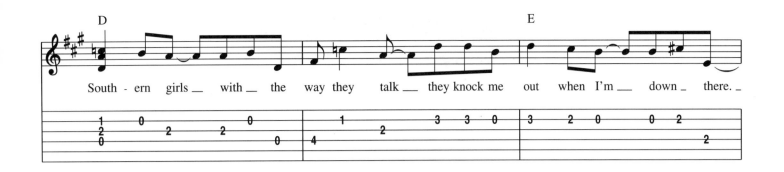

South - ern girls __ with __ the way they talk __ they knock me out when I'm __ down __ there. __

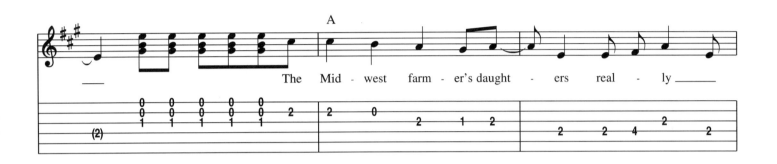

__ The Mid - west farm - er's daught - ers real - ly _____

make you feel al - right. _____ And __ the North - ern girls __ with __ the

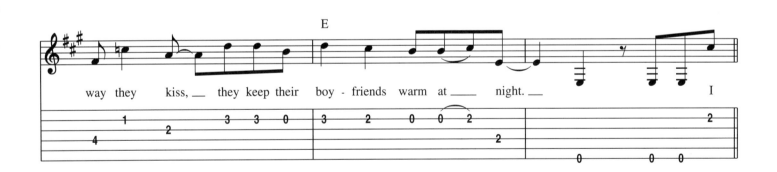

way they kiss, __ they keep their boy - friends warm at _____ night. __

Chorus

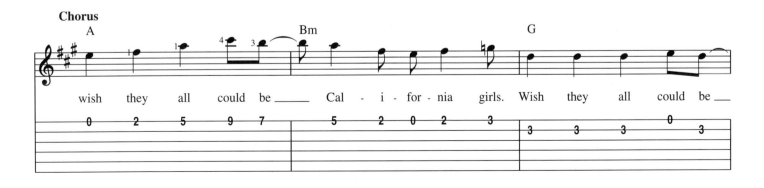

wish they all could be _____ Cal - i - for - nia girls. Wish they all could be __

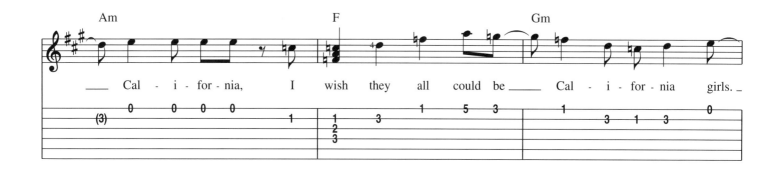

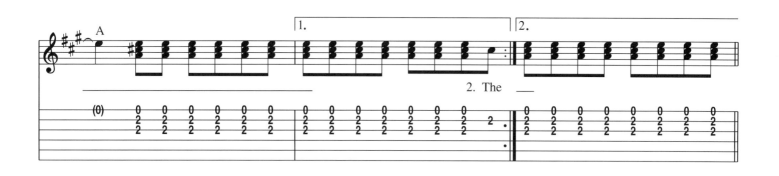

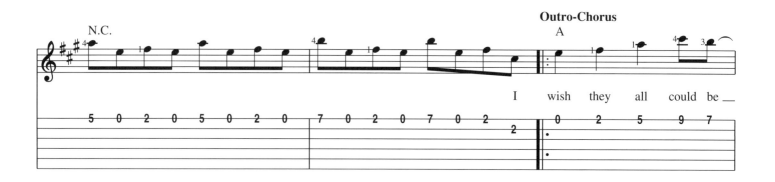

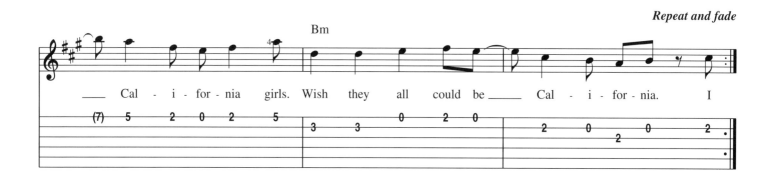

Additional Lyrics

2. The West Coast has the sunshine,
   And the girls all get so tan.
   I dig a French bikini on Hawaiian islands dolls,
   By a palm tree in the sand.
   I been all around this great big world
   And I've seen all kinds of girls.
   Yeah, but I couldn't wait to get back in the states,
   Back to the cutest girls in the world.

Don't Know Why

Words and Music by Jesse Harris

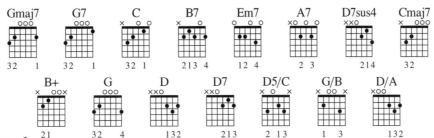

Strum Pattern: 6
Pick Pattern: 4

Intro

Moderately slow

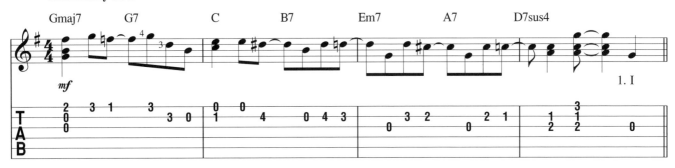

Verse

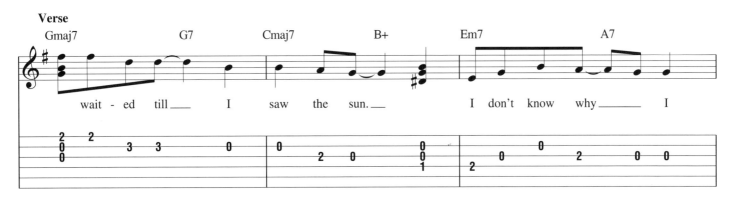

wait-ed till ___ I saw the sun. ___ I don't know why ___ I

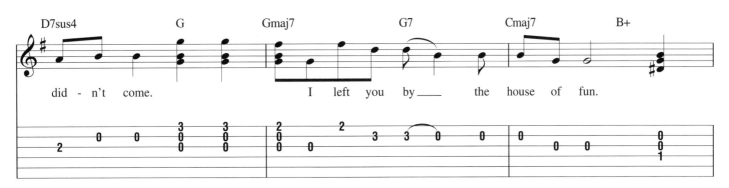

did-n't come. I left you by ___ the house of fun.

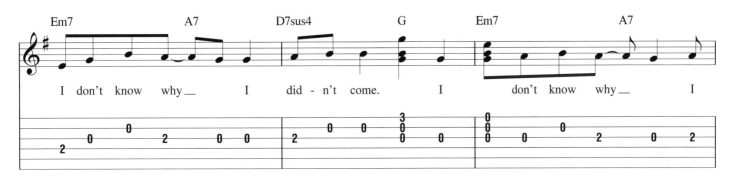

I don't know why ___ I did-n't come. I don't know why ___ I

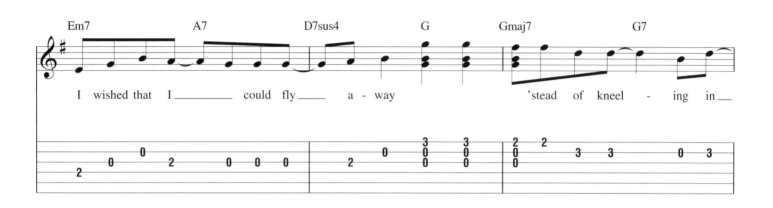

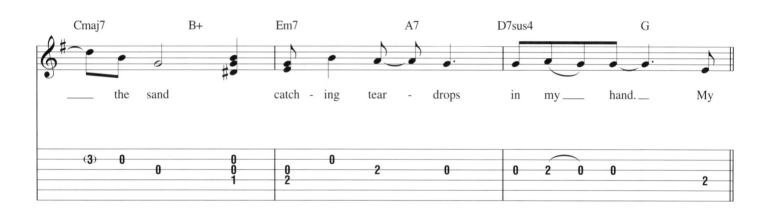

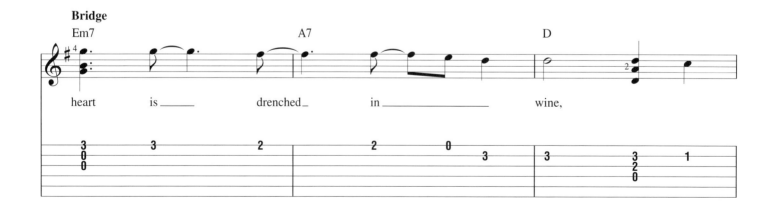

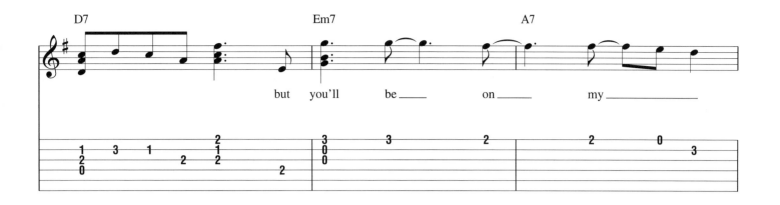

but you'll be ____ on ____ my ____

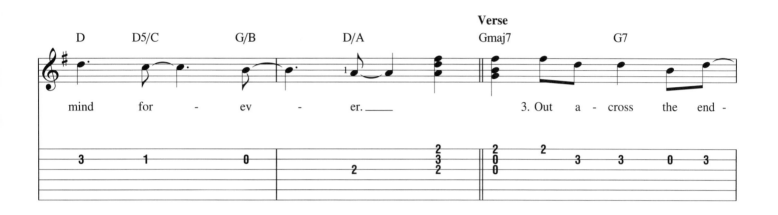

mind for - ev - er. ____ 3. Out a - cross the end -

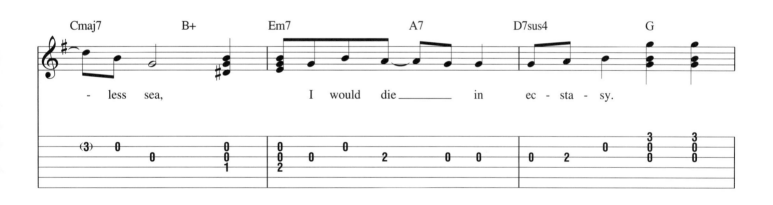

- less sea, I would die ____ in ec - sta - sy.

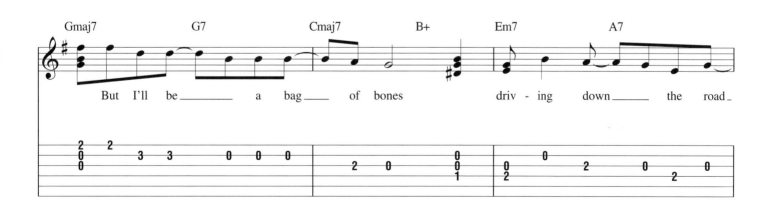

But I'll be ____ a bag ____ of bones driv - ing down ____ the road ____

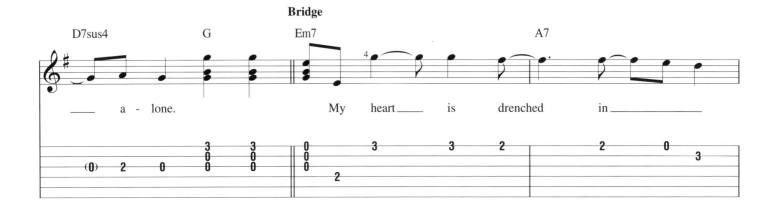

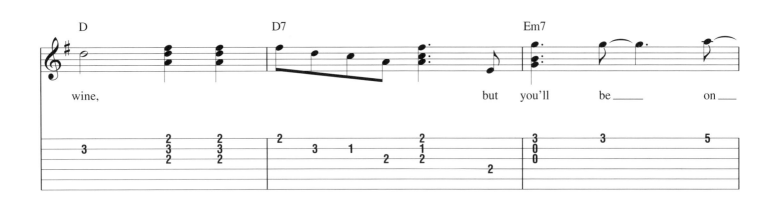

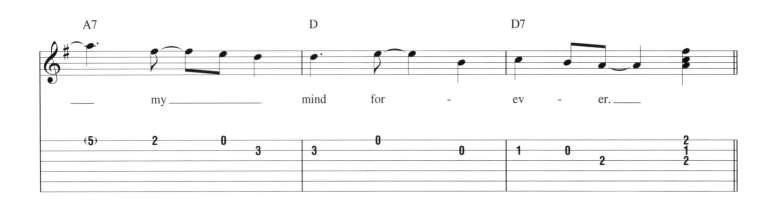

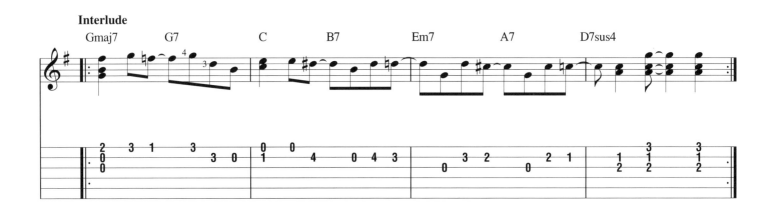

Outro-Verse

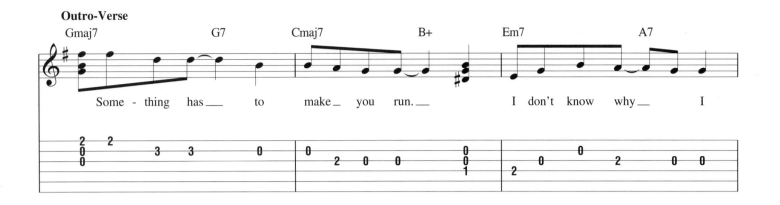

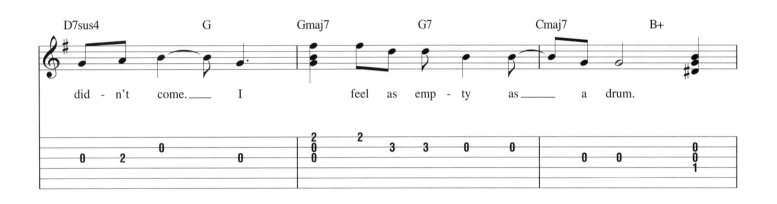

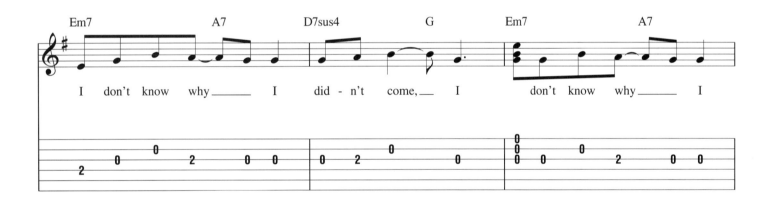

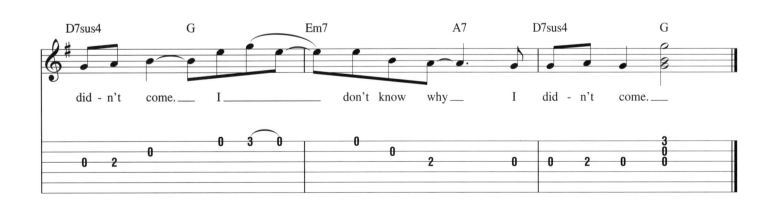

Don't Let the Sun Go Down on Me

Words and Music by Elton John and Bernie Taupin

Strum Pattern: 4, 6
Pick Pattern: 5, 6

Frankenstein

By Edgar Winter

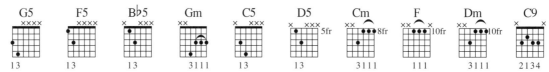

Strum Pattern: 1

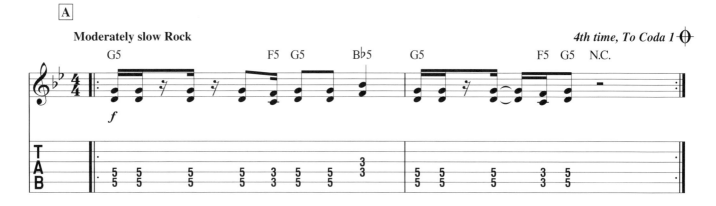

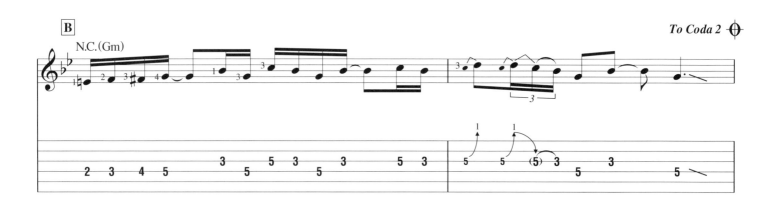

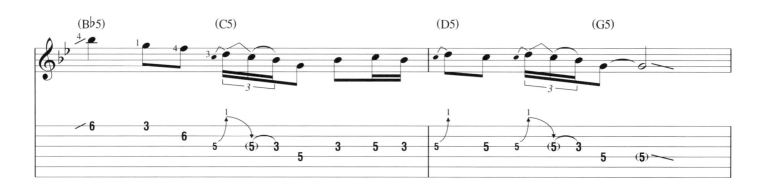

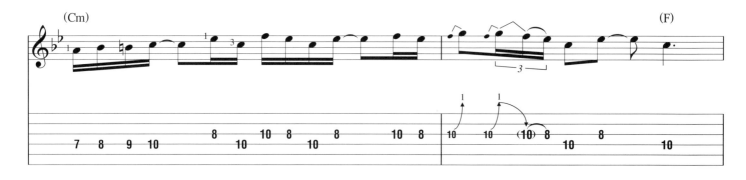

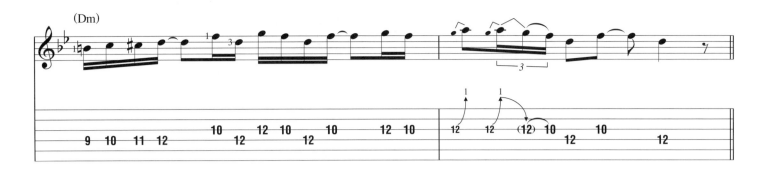

2nd time, D.C. al Coda 1
(take repeat)

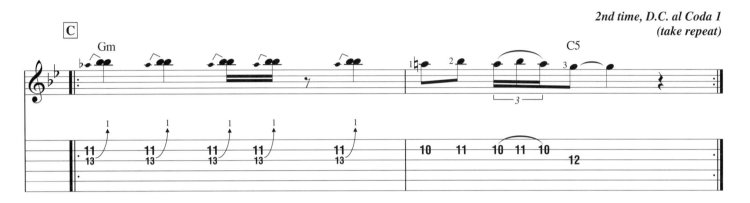

$\oplus$ **Coda 1**

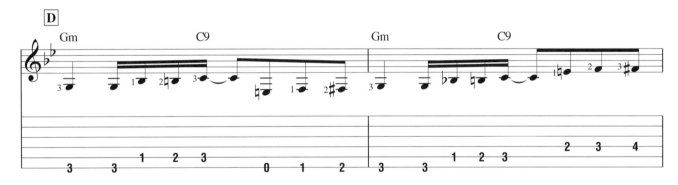

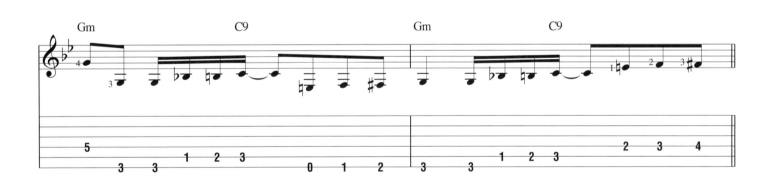

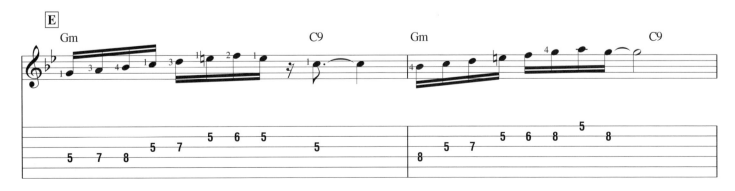

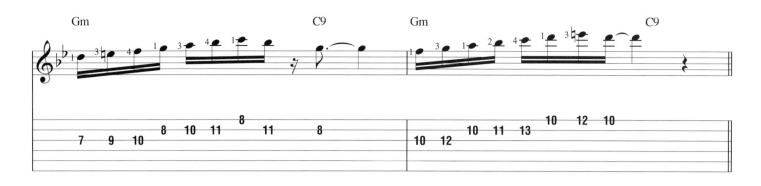

2nd time, D.C. al Coda 2
(take repeat)

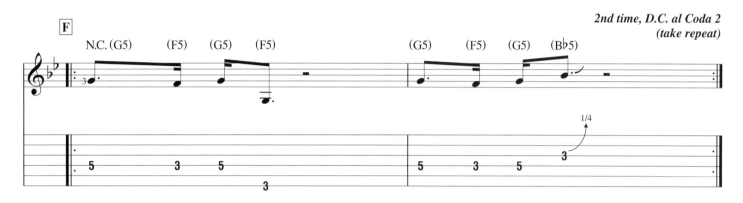

⊕ **Coda 2**

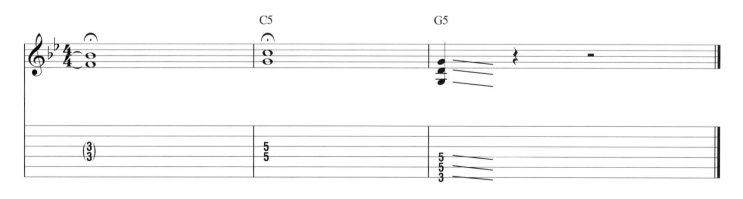

I'm Just Talkin' About Tonight

Words and Music by Scotty Emerick and Toby Keith

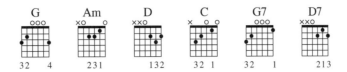

Strum Pattern: 2, 3
Pick Pattern: 3, 4

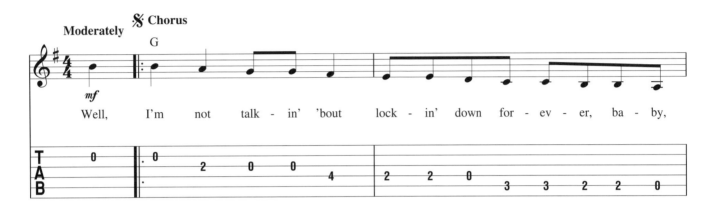

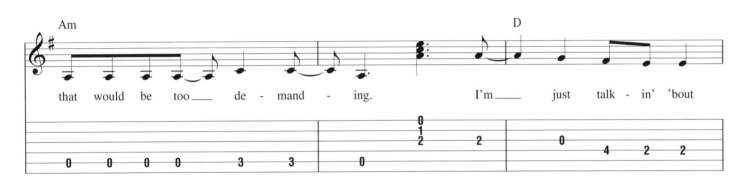

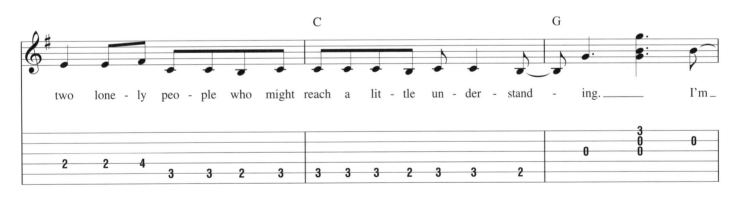

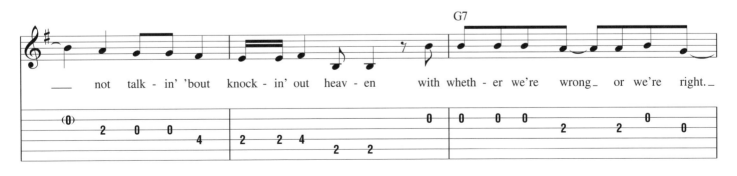

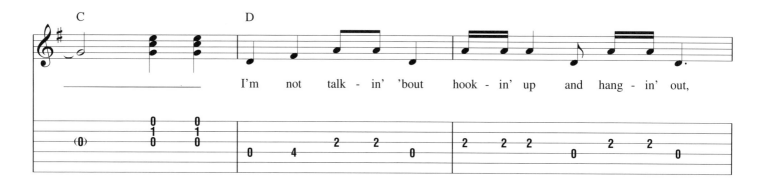

I'm not talk - in' 'bout hook - in' up and hang - in' out,

To Coda

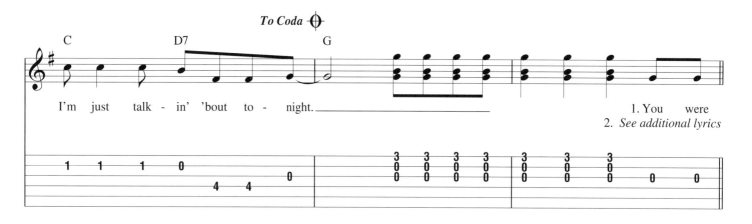

I'm just talk - in' 'bout to - night._____

1. You were
2. *See additional lyrics*

Verse

sit - tin' on your bar - stool, talk - in' to some fool who did - n't have a clue.

I guess he could - n't see you were look - in' right at me, 'cause I was

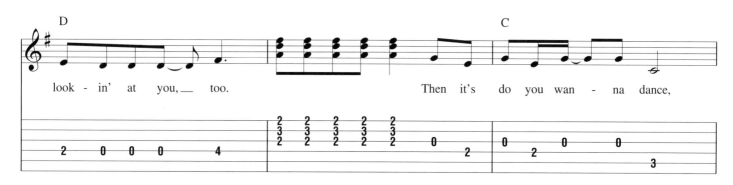

look - in' at you,___ too. Then it's do you wan - na dance,

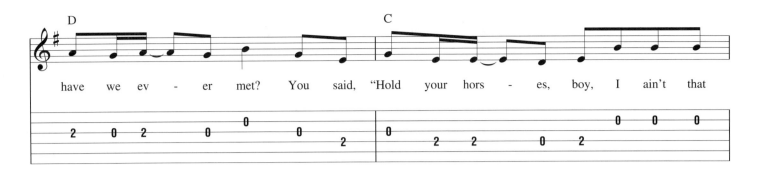

have   we   ev - er   met?   You   said,   "Hold   your   hors - es,   boy,   I   ain't   that

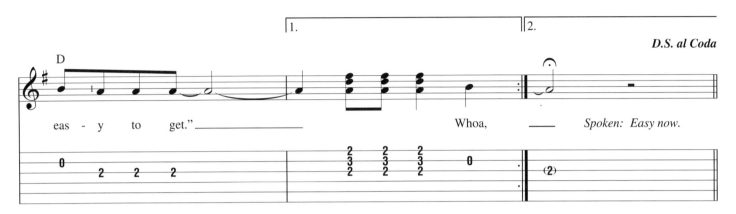

D.S. al Coda

eas - y   to   get." _____   Whoa, ____   *Spoken: Easy now.*

⊕ Coda

Yeah,   I'm   just   talk - in'   'bout

lit - tle   bit   lat - er   to - night. _____

Additional Lyrics

2. She said, "I only take it slow,
   By now you oughta know that I ain't diggin' this.
   If we can start as friends,
   The weekend just might end with a little kiss."
   She said, "I'm a lady lookin' for a man in my life
   Who'll make a good husband, I'll make a good wife."

The Heart of the Matter

Words and Music by John David Souther, Don Henley and Mike Campbell

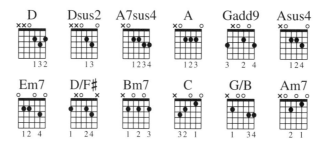

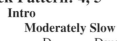

Strum Pattern: 3, 4
Pick Pattern: 4, 5

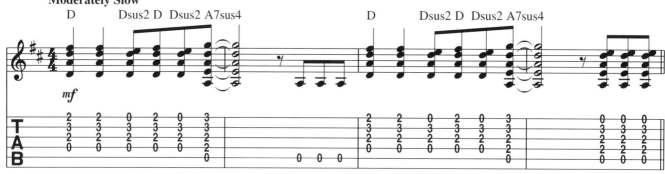

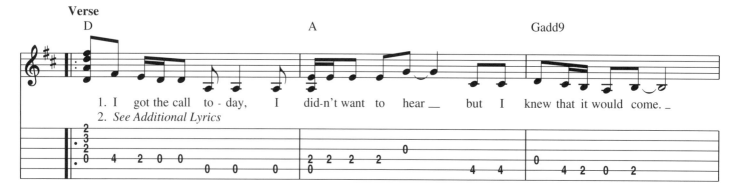

1. I got the call to-day, I did-n't want to hear __ but I knew that it would come. __
2. *See Additional Lyrics*

An old, true friend of ours __ was talk-in' on the phone, __ she said you

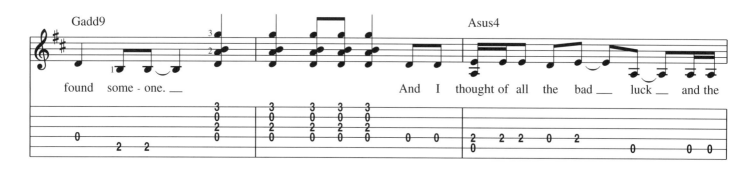

found some-one. __ And I thought of all the bad __ luck __ and the

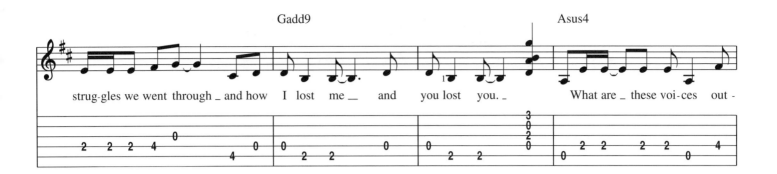

struggles we went through _ and how I lost me _ and you lost you. _ What are _ these voi-ces out-

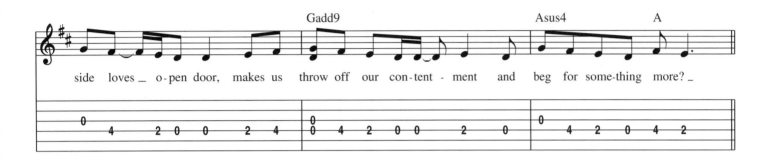

side loves _ o-pen door, makes us throw off our con-tent - ment and beg for some-thing more? _

Pre-Chorus

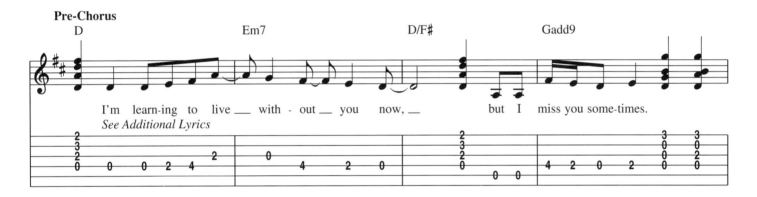

I'm learn-ing to live _ with - out _ you now, _ but I miss you some-times.
See Additional Lyrics

The more I know, _ the less I un-der-stand, _ all the things I thought I knew, _ I'm

𝄋 Chorus

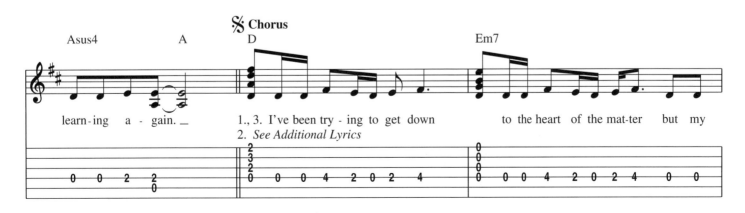

learn-ing a - gain. _ 1., 3. I've been try - ing to get down to the heart of the mat-ter but my
2. *See Additional Lyrics*

will gets weak _ and my thoughts seem to scat-ter but I think it's a-bout for-give-ness,

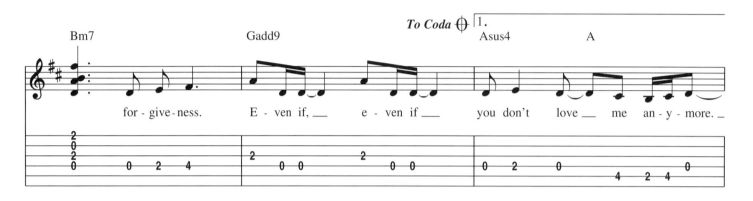

To Coda ⊕ |1.

for-give-ness. E - ven if, __ e - ven if __ you don't love __ me an - y - more. _

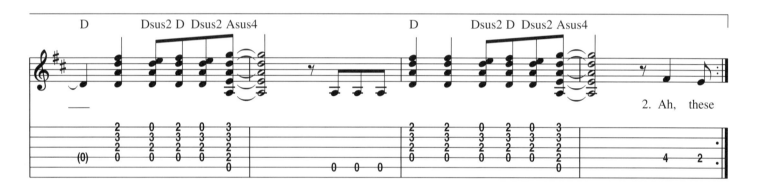

2. Ah, these

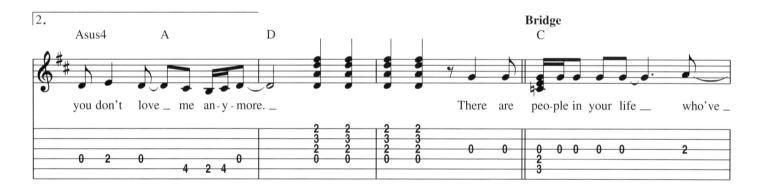

|2.

you don't love _ me an - y - more. _ There are peo-ple in your life __ who've __

Bridge

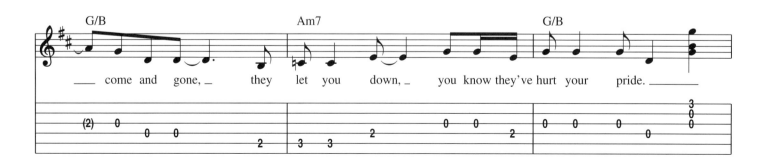

__ come and gone, _ they let you down, _ you know they've hurt your pride. _____

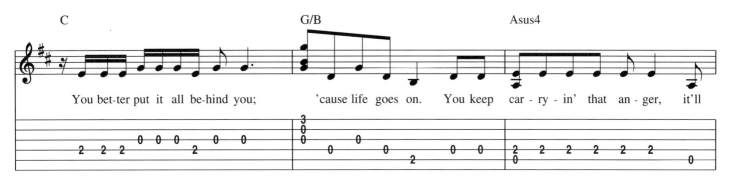

You bet-ter put it all be-hind you; 'cause life goes on. You keep car-ry-in' that an-ger, it'll

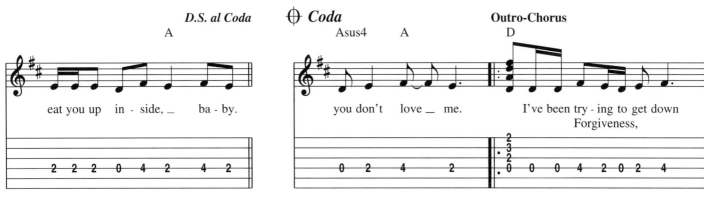

eat you up in-side, _ ba-by.

you don't love _ me. I've been try-ing to get down
Forgiveness,

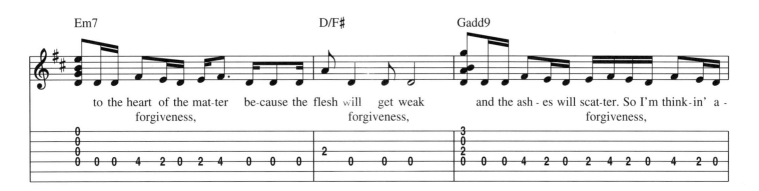

to the heart of the mat-ter be-cause the flesh will get weak and the ash-es will scat-ter. So I'm think-in' a-
forgiveness, forgiveness, forgiveness,

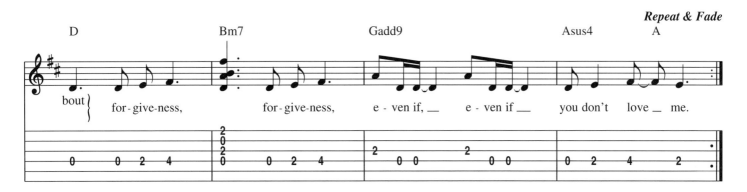

bout for-give-ness, for-give-ness, e-ven if, _ e-ven if __ you don't love _ me.

Additional Lyrics

2. Ah, these times are so uncertain,
   There's a yearning undefined
   ...People filled with rage.
   We all need a little tenderness,
   How can love survive in such a graceless age?
   The trust and self-assurance that led to happiness
   They're the very things we kill, I guess.
   Pride and competition
   Cannot fill these empty arms
   And the work I put between us
   Doesn't keep me warm.

Pre-Chorus I'm learning to live without you now,
   But I miss you, baby.
   The more I know, the less I understand.
   All the things I thought I'd figured out,
   I have to learn again.

Chorus 2. I've been trying to get down
   To the heart of the matter,
   But everything changes
   And my friends seem to scatter.
   But I think it's about forgiveness, forgiveness.
   Even if, even if you don't love me anymore.

Hide Away

By Freddie King and Sonny Thompson

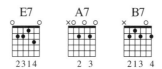

Strum Pattern: 3
Pick Pattern: 4

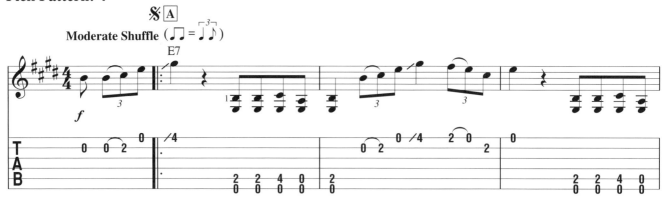

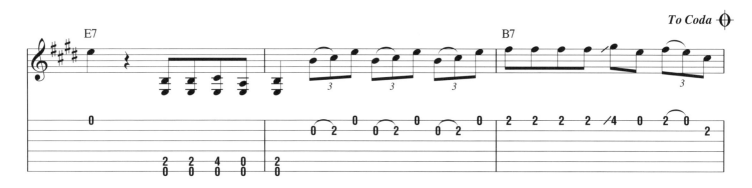

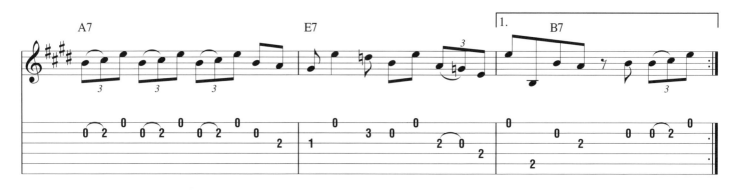

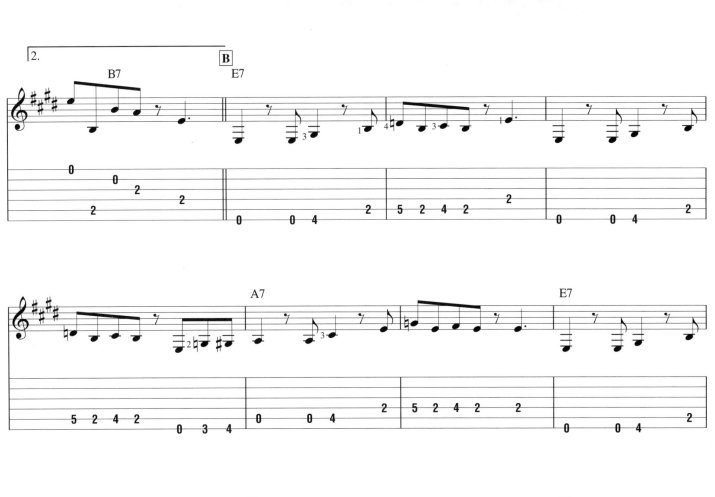

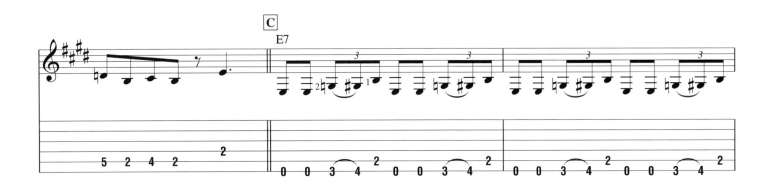

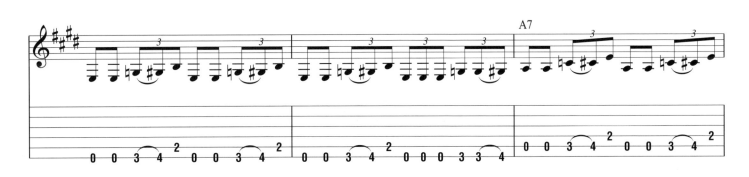

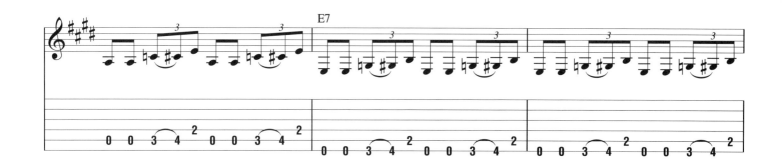

D

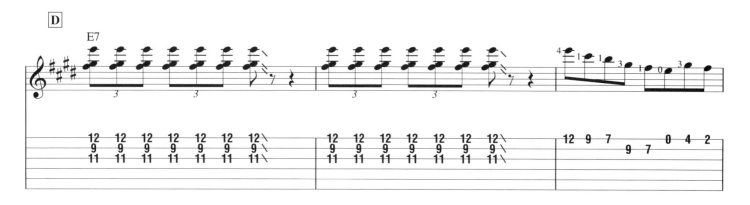

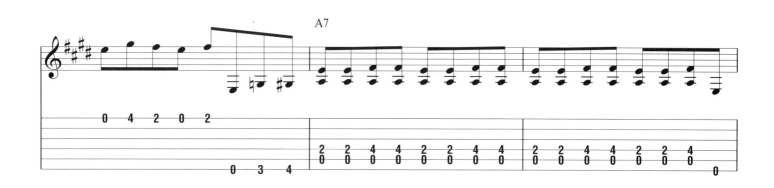

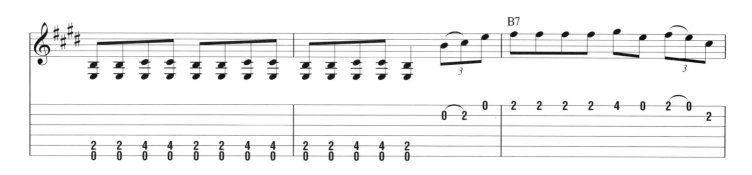

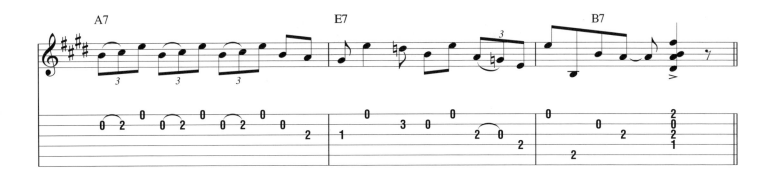

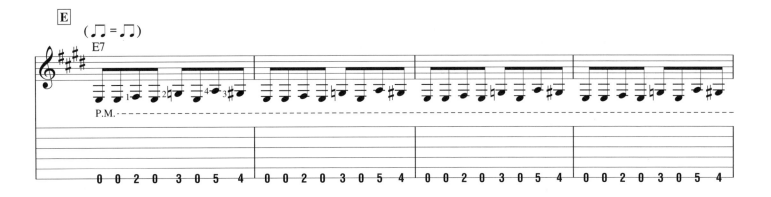

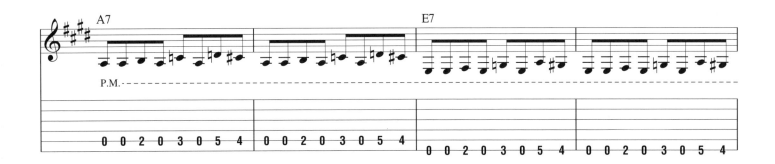

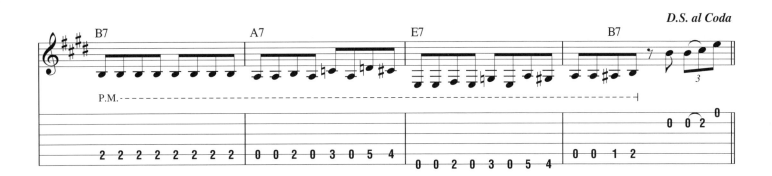

*Played as even eighth notes.

How Insensitive
(Insensatez)

Music by Antonio Carlos Jobim
Original Words by Vinicius de Moraes
English Words by Norman Gimbel

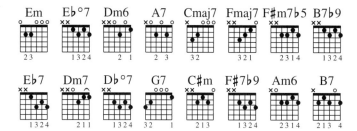

Strum Pattern: 3
Pick Pattern: 3

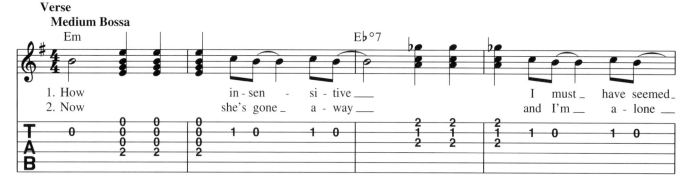

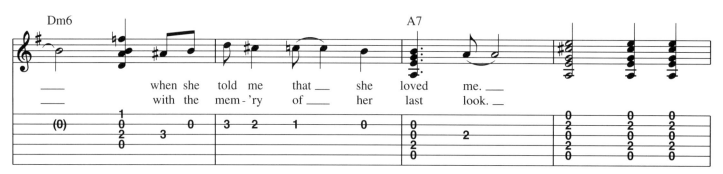

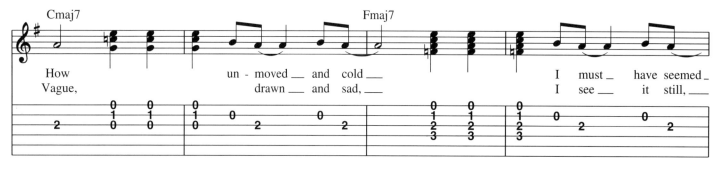

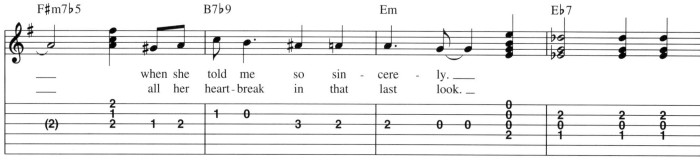

Lucy in the Sky With Diamonds

Words and Music by John Lennon and Paul McCartney

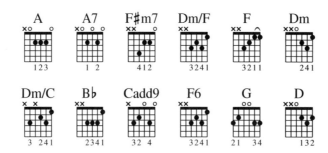

Strum Pattern: 8, 9
Pick Pattern: 7, 8

*Tempo 1 on repeats

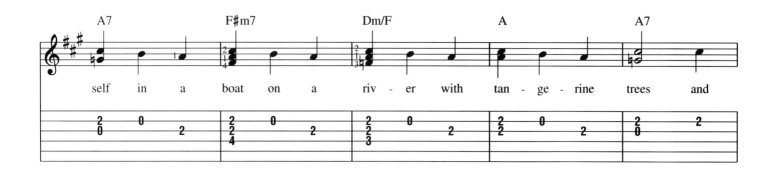

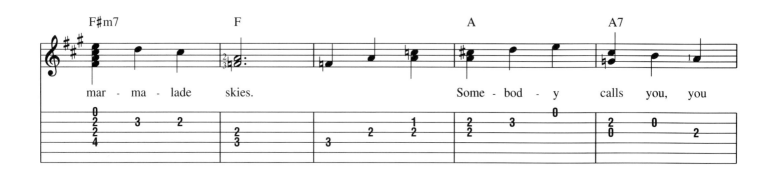

F#m7 | Dm/F | A | A7 | F#m7

an - swer quite slow - ly, _____ a girl with ka - lei - do - scope eyes. _____

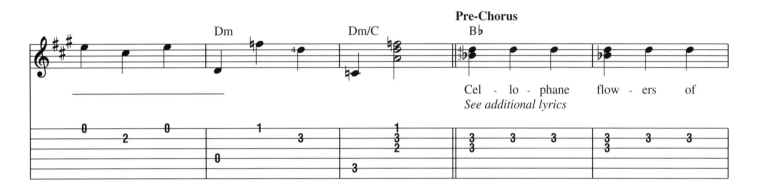

Dm | Dm/C | **Pre-Chorus** B♭

_____ Cel - lo - phane flow - ers of
See additional lyrics

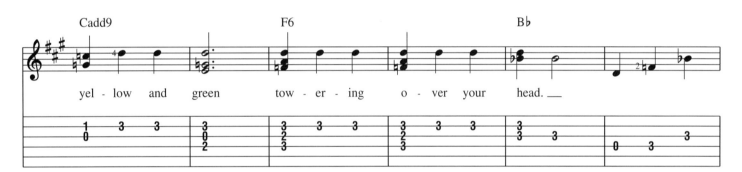

Cadd9 | F6 | B♭

yel - low and green tow - er - ing o - ver your head. __

Strum Pattern: 2, 5
Pick Pattern: 1, 4

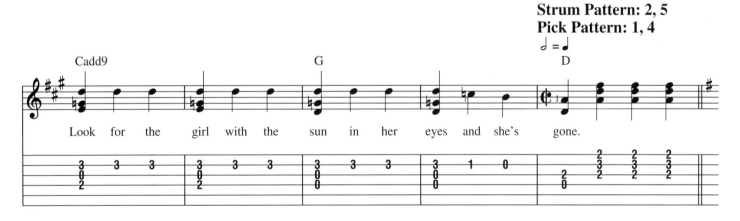

Cadd9 | G | D

Look for the girl with the sun in her eyes and she's gone.

Chorus
G | C | D | G | C

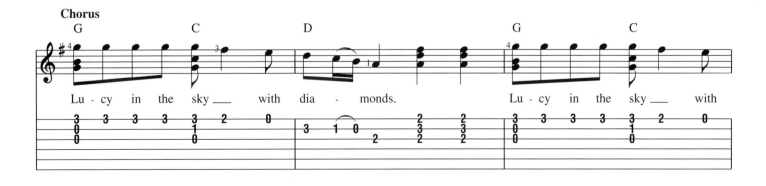

Lu - cy in the sky __ with dia - monds. Lu - cy in the sky __ with

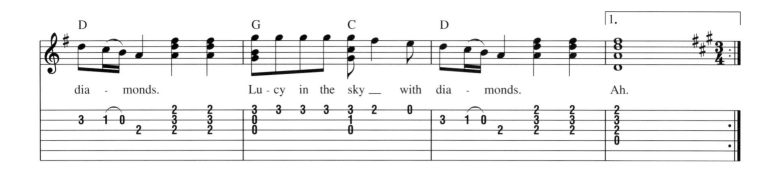

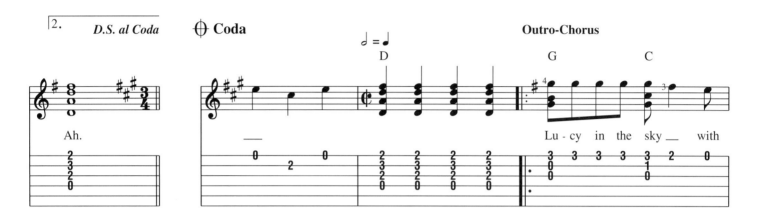

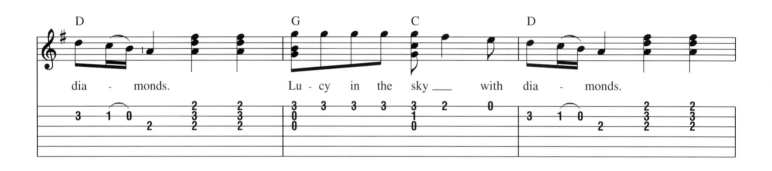

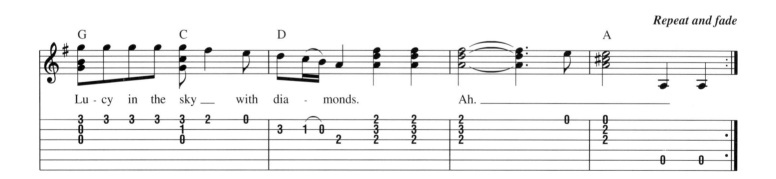

Additional Lyrics

2. Follow her down to a bridge by a fountain
Where rocking horse people eat marshmallow pies.
Ev'ryone smiles as you drift past the flowers
That grow so incredibly high.

Pre-Chorus Newspaper taxis appear on the shore
Waiting to take you away.
Climb in the back with your
Head in the clouds and you're gone.

3. Picture yourself on a train in a station
With plasticine porters with looking-glass ties.
Suddenly someone is there at the turnstile,
The girl with kaleidoscope eyes.

No Woman No Cry

Words and Music by Vincent Ford

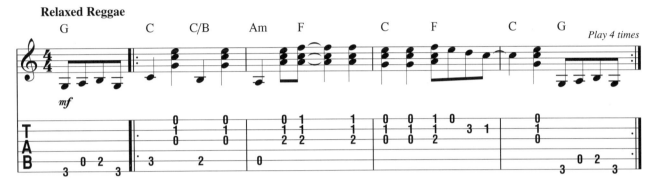

Strum Pattern: 3

Intro

Relaxed Reggae

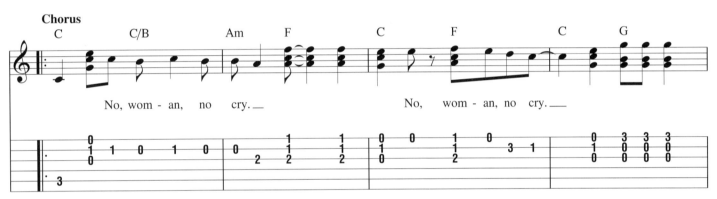

Chorus

No, wom-an, no cry.___   No, wom-an, no cry.___

No, wom-an, no cry.
Here,___ lit-tle dar-lin', don't shed no tears.

No, wom-an, no cry.___

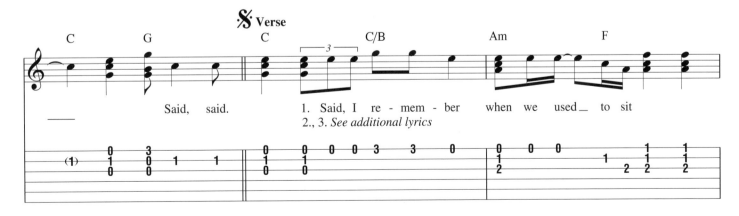

Verse

Said, said.   1. Said, I re-mem-ber when we used_ to sit

2., 3. *See additional lyrics*

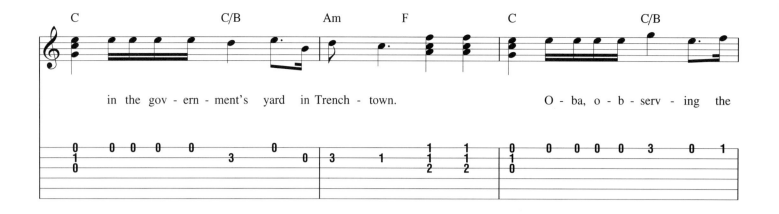

in the gov - ern - ment's yard in Trench - town. O - ba, o - b - serv - ing the

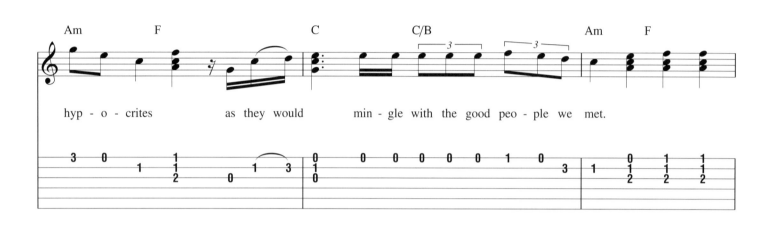

hyp - o - crites as they would min - gle with the good peo - ple we met.

Good friends we had,___ oh good friends we've lost___ a - long the way.___

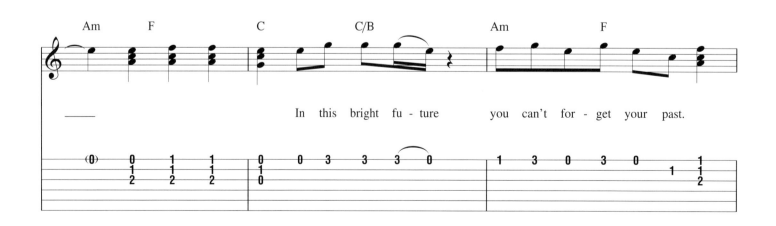

___ In this bright fu - ture you can't for - get your past.

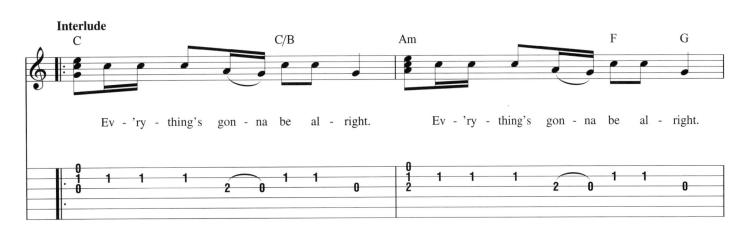

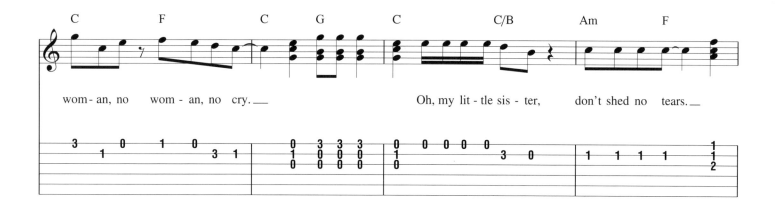

wom-an, no wom-an, no cry.___ Oh, my lit-tle sis-ter, don't shed no tears.___

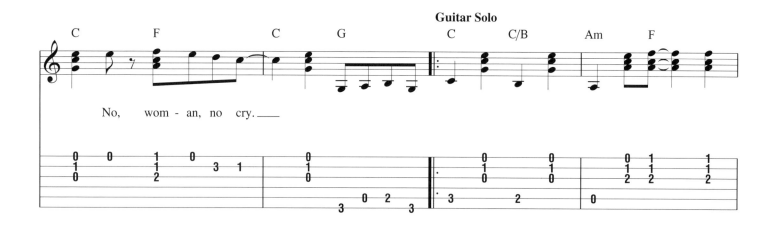

Guitar Solo

No, wom-an, no cry.___

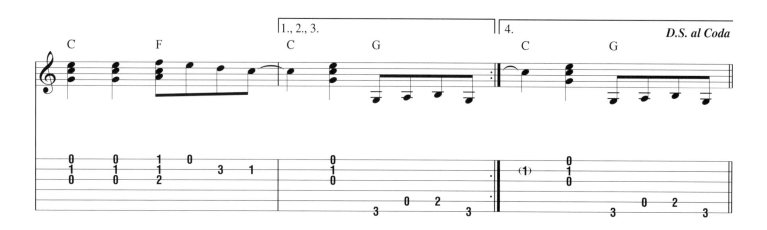

1., 2., 3.   4.   *D.S. al Coda*

Coda

Chorus

___through, but while I'm gone I mean... No, wom-an, no cry.___

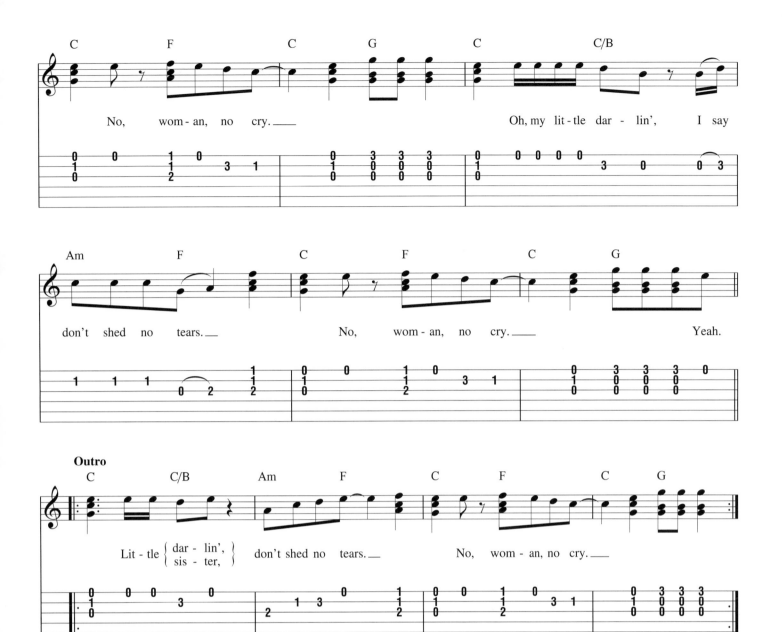

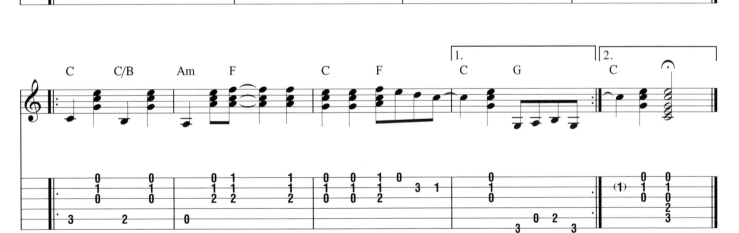

Additional Lyrics

2., 3. Said I remember when we used to sit
In the government's yard in Trenchtown.
And then Georgie would make a firelight
As it was logwood burnin' through the night.
Then we would cook corn meal porridge
Of which I'll share with you.
My feet is my only carriage,
So, I've got to push on through, but while I'm gone I mean...

Respect

Words and Music by Otis Redding

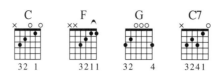

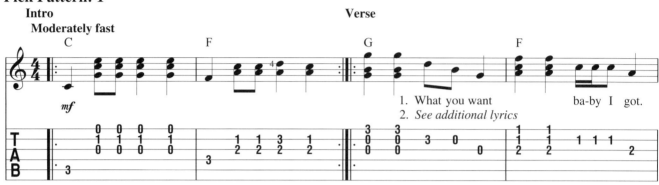

Strum Pattern: 5
Pick Pattern: 1

Intro
Moderately fast

Verse

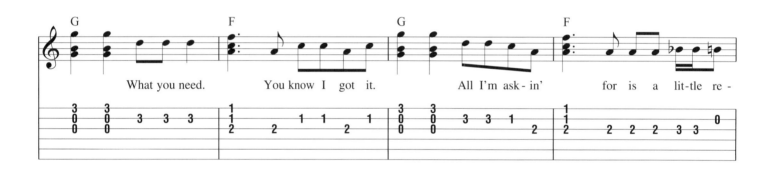

1. What you want   ba-by I got.
2. *See additional lyrics*

What you need.   You know I got it.   All I'm ask-in'   for is a lit-tle re-

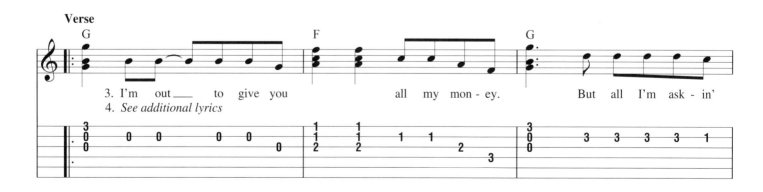

spect, when you come home.   Ba-by,   when you come home,   re-spect.

Verse

3. I'm out___ to give you   all my mon-ey.   But all I'm ask-in'
4. *See additional lyrics*

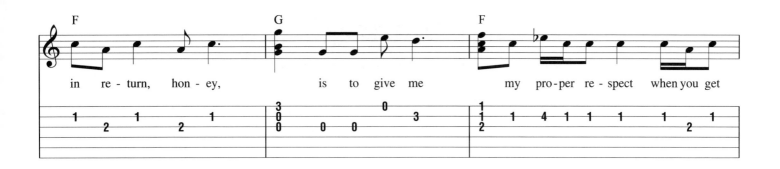

in re-turn, hon-ey, is to give me my pro-per re-spect when you get

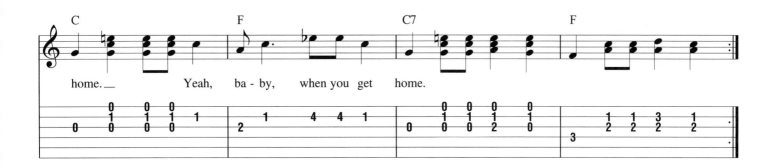

home.___ Yeah, ba-by, when you get home.

Chorus

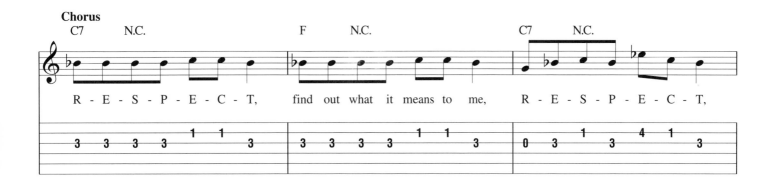

R-E-S-P-E-C-T, find out what it means to me, R-E-S-P-E-C-T,

Outro

Repeat and fade

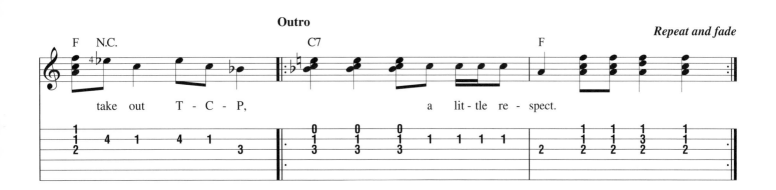

take out T-C-P, a lit-tle re-spect.

Additional Lyrics

2. I ain't gonna do you wrong
   While you gone.
   I ain't gonna do you wrong
   'Cause I don't wanna.
   All I'm askin' is for a little respect,
   When you come home.
   Baby, when you come home,
   Respect.

4. Ooh, your kisses,
   Sweeter than honey,
   But guess what,
   So here's my money.
   All I want you to do for me
   Is give me some here when you get home.
   Yeah, baby, when you get home.

Sharp Dressed Man

Words and Music by Billy F Gibbons, Dusty Hill and Frank Beard

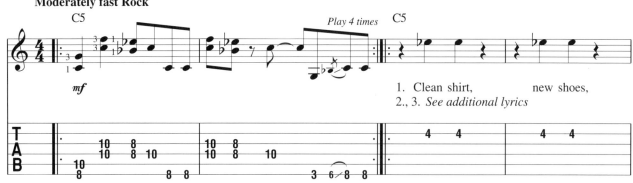

Strum Pattern: 1, 2

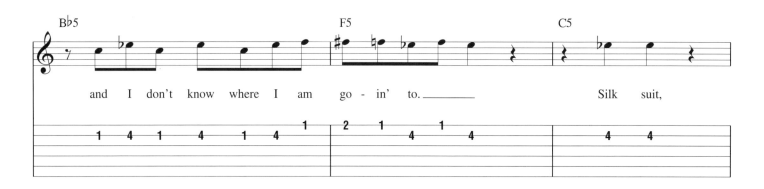

1. Clean shirt,   new shoes,
2., 3. *See additional lyrics*

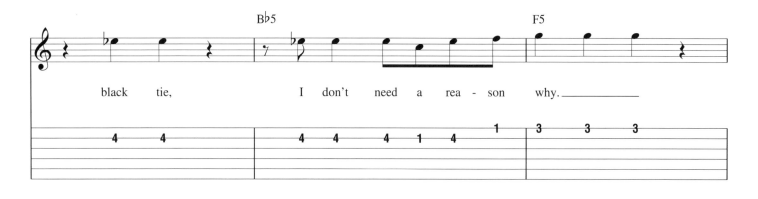

and I don't know where I am go - in' to. _____   Silk suit,

black tie,   I don't need a rea - son why. _____

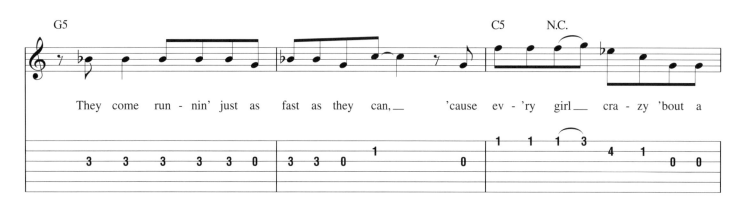

They come run - nin' just as fast as they can, __   'cause ev - 'ry girl __ cra - zy 'bout a

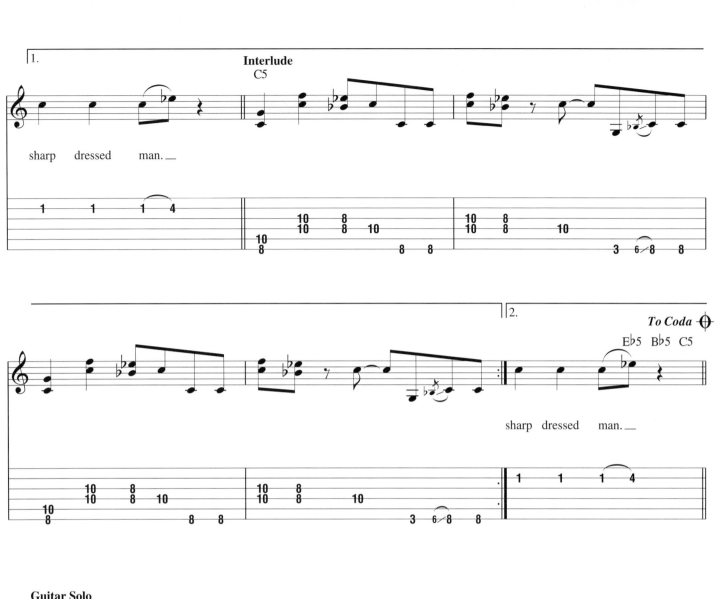

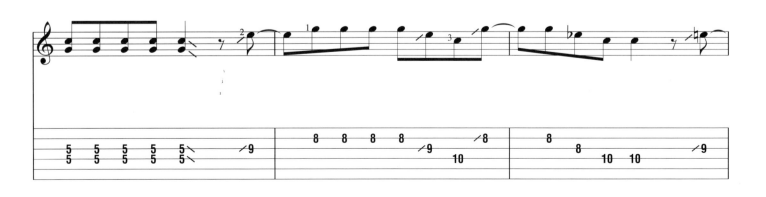

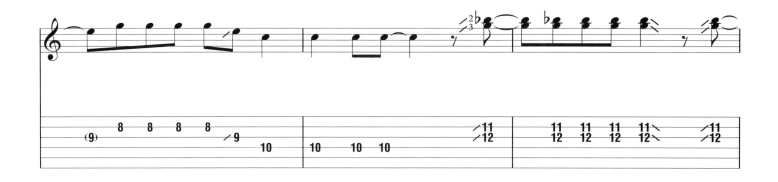

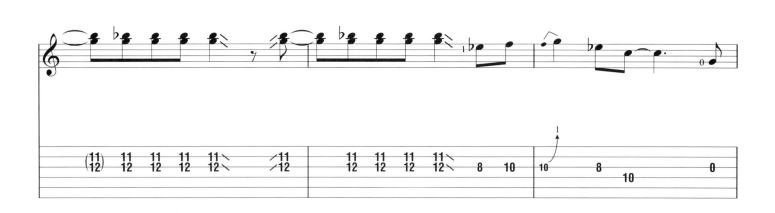

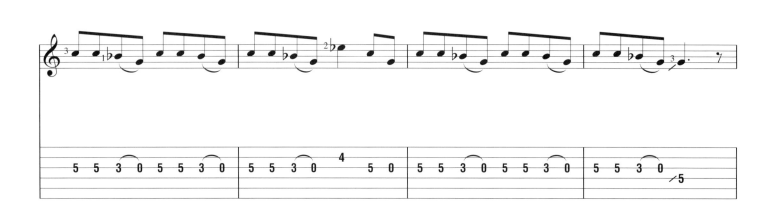

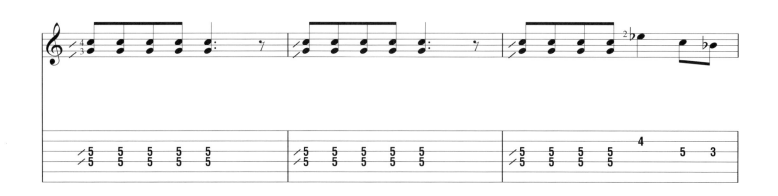

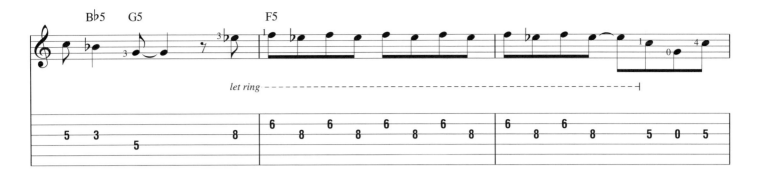

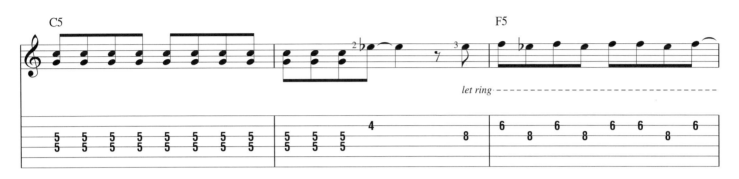

D.C. al Coda
(take 2nd ending)

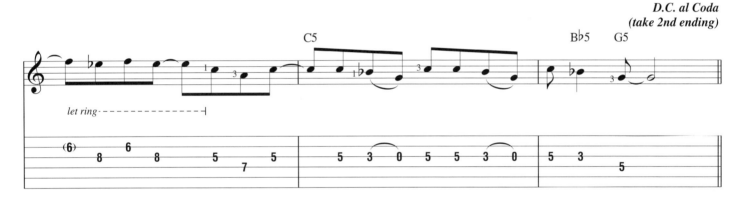

Coda
Outro

Repeat and fade

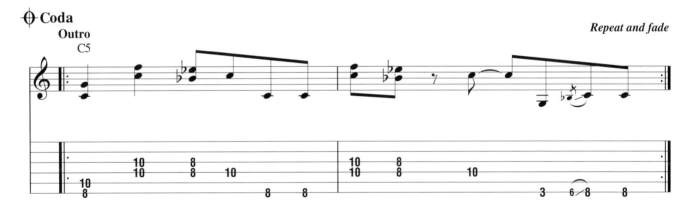

Additional Lyrics

2. Gold watch, diamond ring,
   I ain't missin' not a single thing.
   Cuff links, stick pin,
   When I step out I'm gonna do you in.
   They come runnin' just as fast as they can,
   'Cause every girl crazy 'bout a sharp dressed man.

3. Top coat, top hat,
   I don't worry 'cause my wallet's fat.
   Black shades, white gloves,
   Lookin' sharp, lookin' for love.
   They come runnin' just as fast as they can,
   'Cause every girl crazy 'bout a sharp dressed man.

(Sittin' On)
The Dock of the Bay

Words and Music by Steve Cropper and Otis Redding

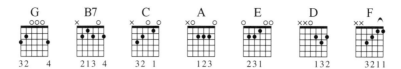

Strum Pattern: 2
Pick Pattern: 2

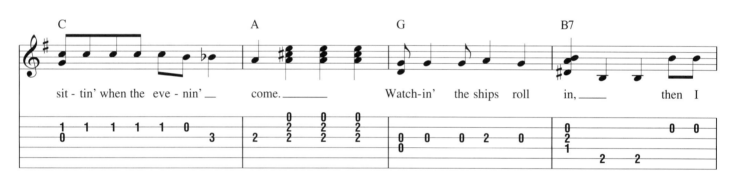

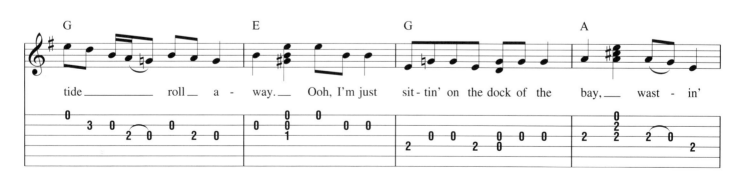

Additional Lyrics

2. I left my home in Georgia,
   Headed for the Frisco bay.
   I have nothin' to live for,
   Look like nothin's gonna come my way.

3. Sittin' here restin' my bones,
   And this loneliness won't leave me alone.
   Two thousand miles I roam,
   Just to make this dock my home.

Southern Cross

Words and Music by Stephen Stills, Richard Curtis and Michael Curtis

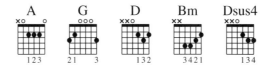

Strum Pattern: 5
Pick Pattern: 6

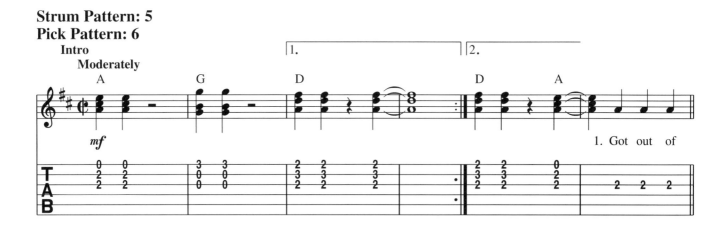

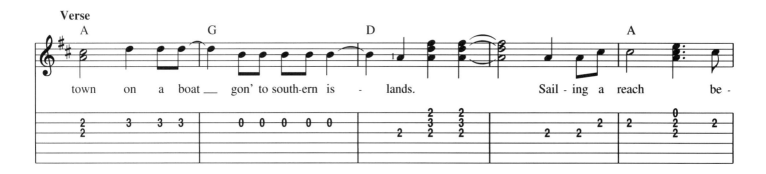

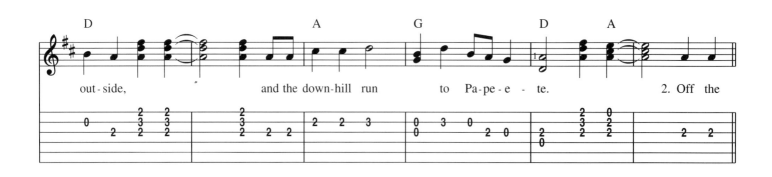

Verse

wind on this hea-ding, lie ___ the Mar - que - sas.   We got eight - y feet _ of

4. *See Additional Lyrics*

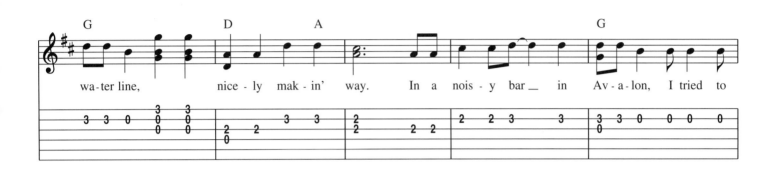

wa-ter line,   nice - ly mak - in' way.   In a nois - y bar _ in Av - a - lon, I tried to

call you,   but on the mid-night watch I re - al - ized   why twice you ran a - way. _

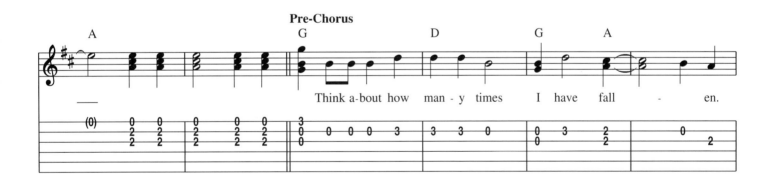

Pre-Chorus

___   Think a-bout how man - y times   I have fall - en.

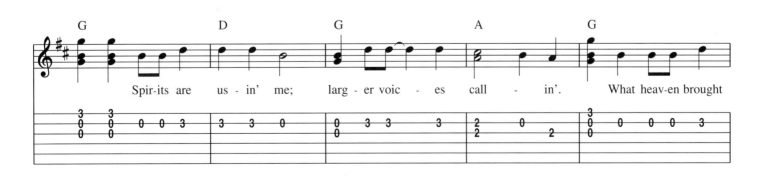

Spir-its are us - in' me; larg - er voic - es call - in'.   What heav-en brought

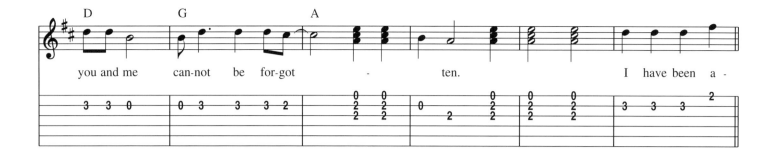

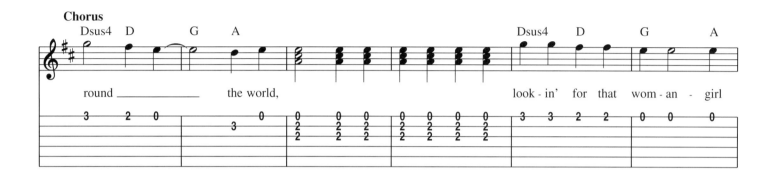

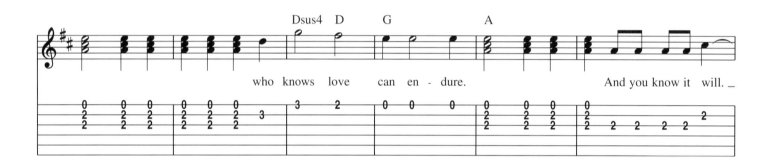

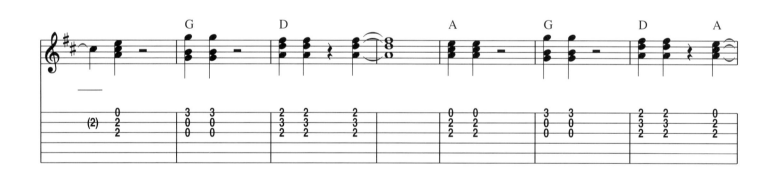

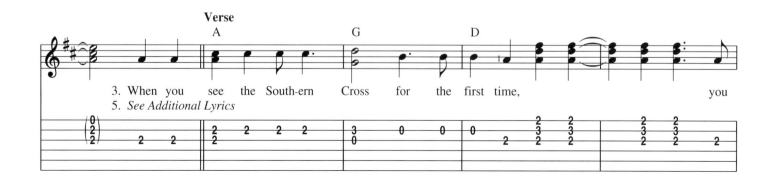

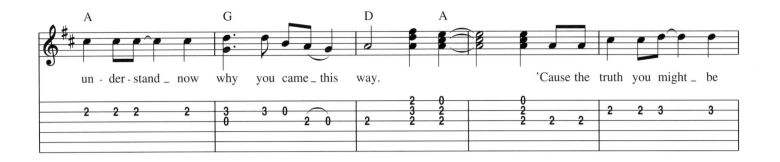

un - der - stand _ now   why   you came _ this   way.   'Cause the truth you might _ be

run - nin'   from   is   so small,   but it's as   big   as   the prom - ise, __   the

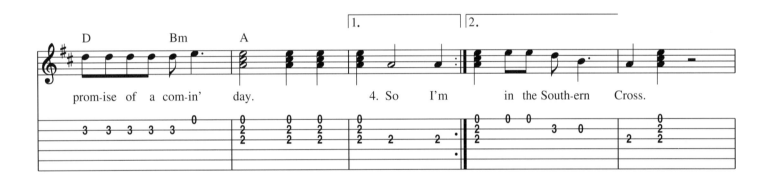

prom - ise of a com - in'   day.   4. So   I'm   in the South - ern   Cross.

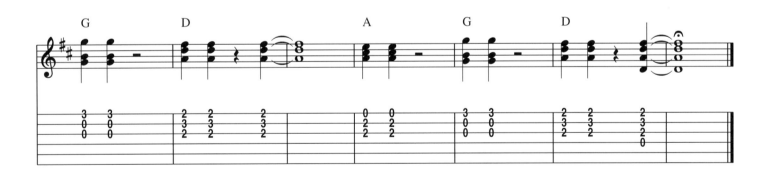

Additional Lyrics

4. So I'm sailing for tomorrow. My dreams are a-dying.
   And my love is an anchor tied to you, tied with a silver chain.
   I have my ship, and all her flags are a-flying.
   She is all that I have left, and music is her name.

5. So we cheated and we lied and we tested.
   And we never failed to fail; it was the easiest thing to do.
   You will survive being bested.
   Somebody fine will come along, make me forget about loving you
   In the Southern Cross.

Uptown Girl

Words and Music by Billy Joel

What'd I Say

Words and Music by Ray Charles

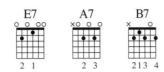

Strum Pattern: 2
Pick Pattern: 4

Intro
Bright Rock

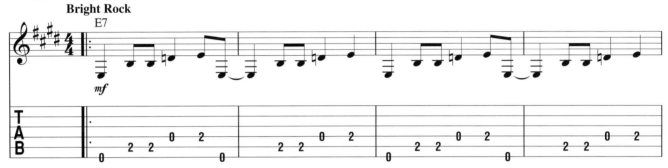

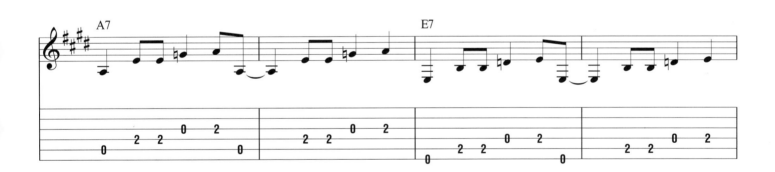

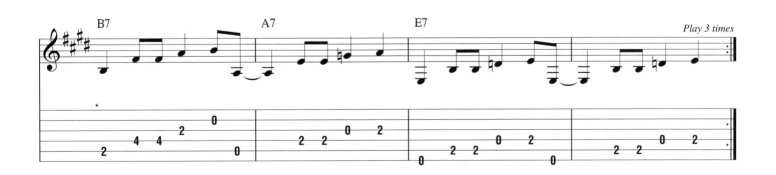

Verse

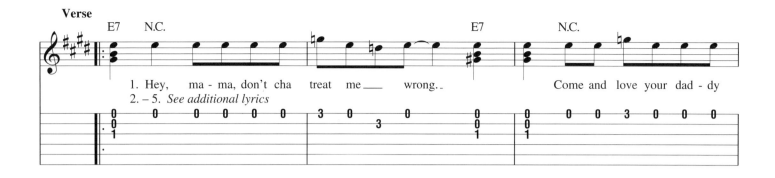

1. Hey, ma - ma, don't cha treat me wrong. Come and love your dad - dy
2. – 5. *See additional lyrics*

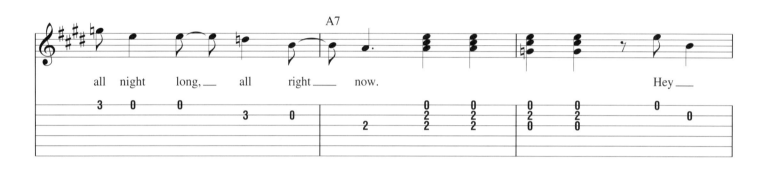

all night long, all right now. Hey

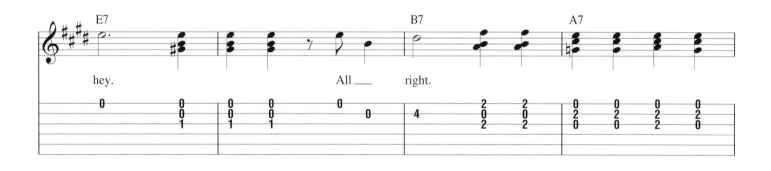

hey. All right.

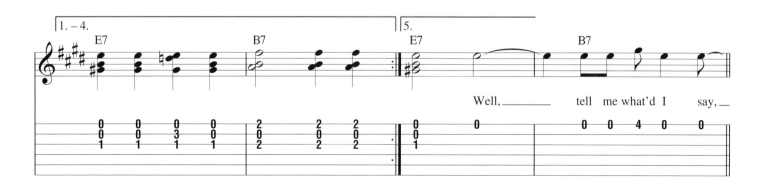

Well, tell me what'd I say,

126

Outro

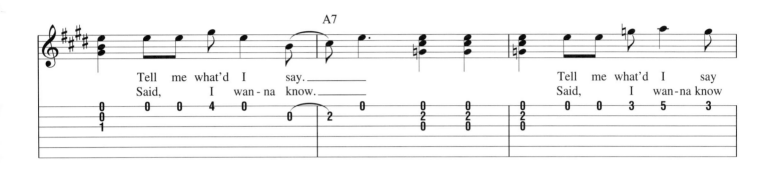

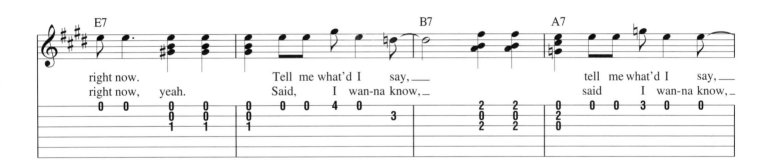

Additional Lyrics

2. See the girl with the diamond ring.
   She knows how to shake that thing.
   All right now. Hey, hey. Hey, hey.

3. Tell your mama, tell your pa.
   I'm gonna send you back to Arkansas.
   Oh yes, ma'm. You don't do right. Don't do right.

4. When you see me in misery,
   Come on, baby see about me now, yeah,
   Hey, hey. All right.

5. See the girl with the red dress on.
   She can do the birdland all night long.
   Oh yeah, yeah. What'd I say? All right.

Where Were You
(When the World Stopped Turning)

Words and Music by Alan Jackson

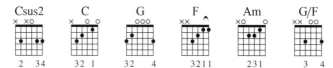

Strum Pattern: 3, 4
Pick Pattern: 2, 5

Intro
Moderately

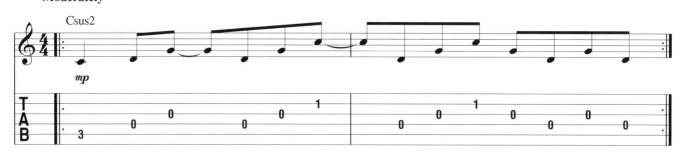

1., 2. Where were you when the world___ stopped turn - in' that Sep - tem - ber

day? ___ Out in the yard___ with your wife and chil - dren or
Teach - in' a class full of in - no - cent chil - dren or

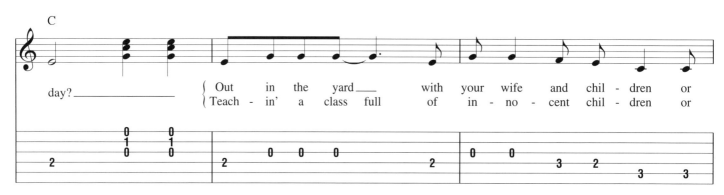

work - in' on some stage___ in L. A.? Did you stand there in shock at the
driv - in' on some cold___ in - ter - state? Did you feel guilt - y 'cause

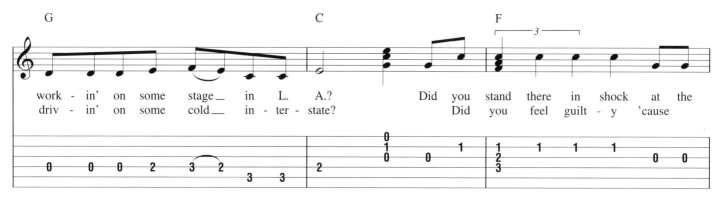

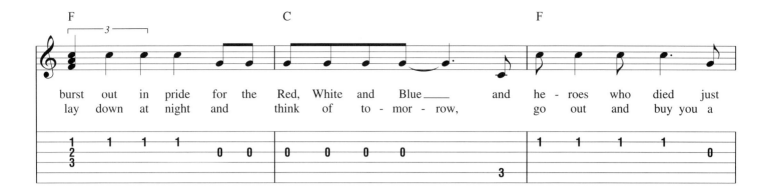

To Coda ⊕

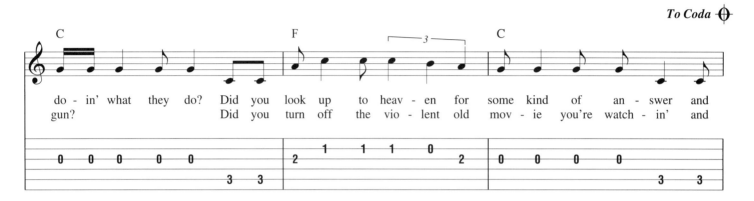

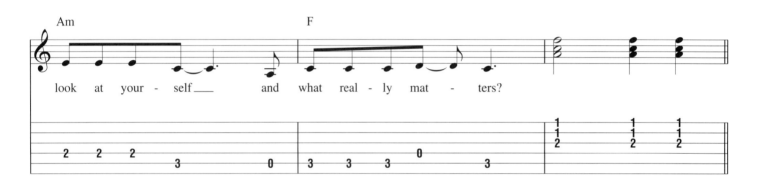

Chorus

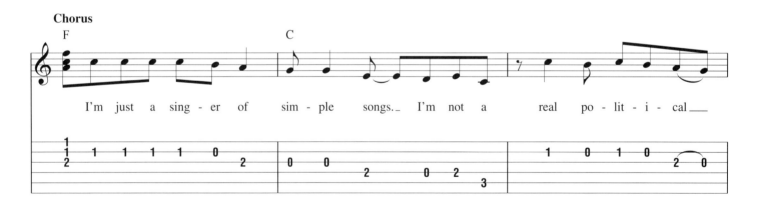

130

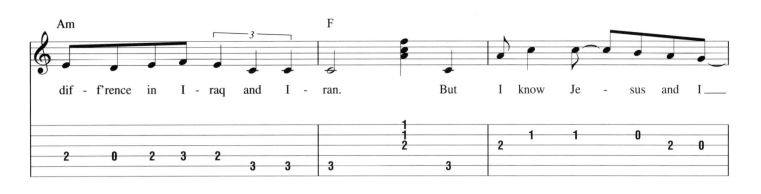

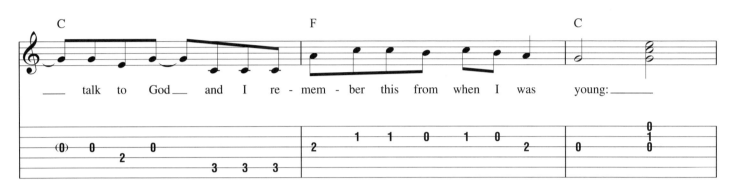

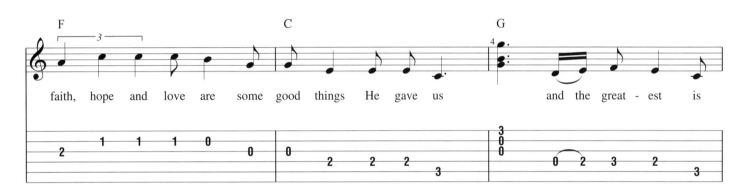

D.S. al Coda

Coda

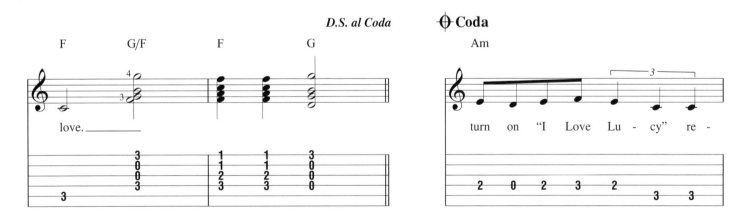

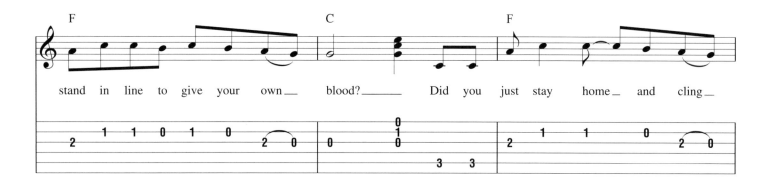

stand in line to give your own ___ blood? ___ Did you just stay home ___ and cling ___

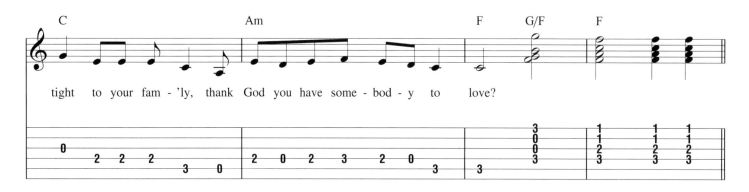

tight to your fam - 'ly, thank God you have some - bod - y to love?

Chorus

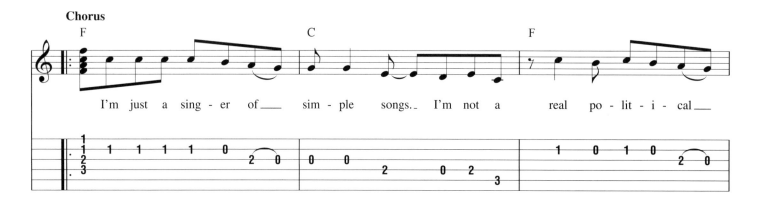

I'm just a sing - er of ___ sim - ple songs. _ I'm not a real po - lit - i - cal ___

man. I watch C N N, ___ but I'm not ___ sure I can tell you the

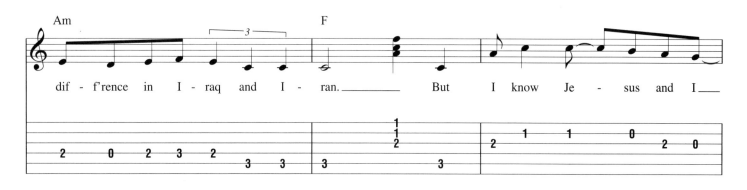

dif - f'rence in I - raq and I - ran. ___ But I know Je - sus and I ___

132

___ talk to God__ and I re - mem - ber this from when I was young:_

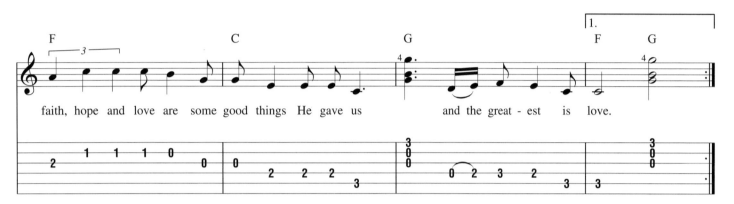

faith, hope and love are some good things He gave us and the great - est is love.

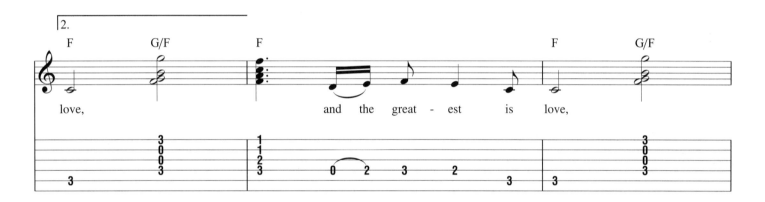

love, and the great - est is love,

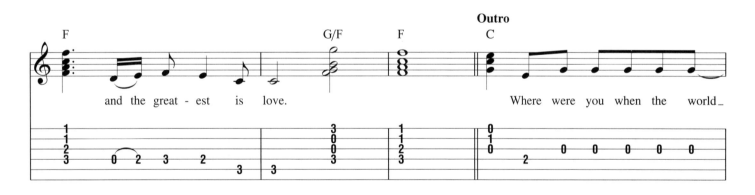

Outro

_and the great - est is love. Where were you when the world__

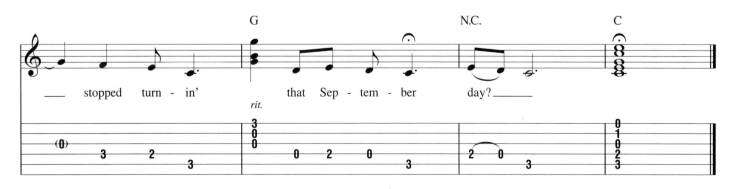

___ stopped turn - in' that Sep - tem - ber day?_____

All I Ask of You

from THE PHANTOM OF THE OPERA
Music by Andrew Lloyd Webber
Lyrics by Charles Hart
Additional Lyrics by Richard Stilgoe

Strum Pattern: 1, 2
Pick Pattern: 2, 4

Additional Lyrics

2. Let me be your shelter, let me be your light;
You're safe, no one will find you, your fears are far behind you.
All I want is freedom, a world with no more night;
And you, always beside me, to hold me and to hide me. Then...

Chorus 2. Then say you'll share with me one love one lifetime.
Let me lead you from your solitude.
Say you need me with you, here, beside you.
Anywhere you go, let me go too.
Christine, that's all I ask of you.

Chorus 3. All I ask for is one love one lifetime.
Say the word and I will follow you.
Share each day with me each night, each morning.
Say you love me! You know I do.
Love me, that's all I ask of you.

(They Long to Be) Close to You

Lyric by Hal David
Music by Burt Bacharach

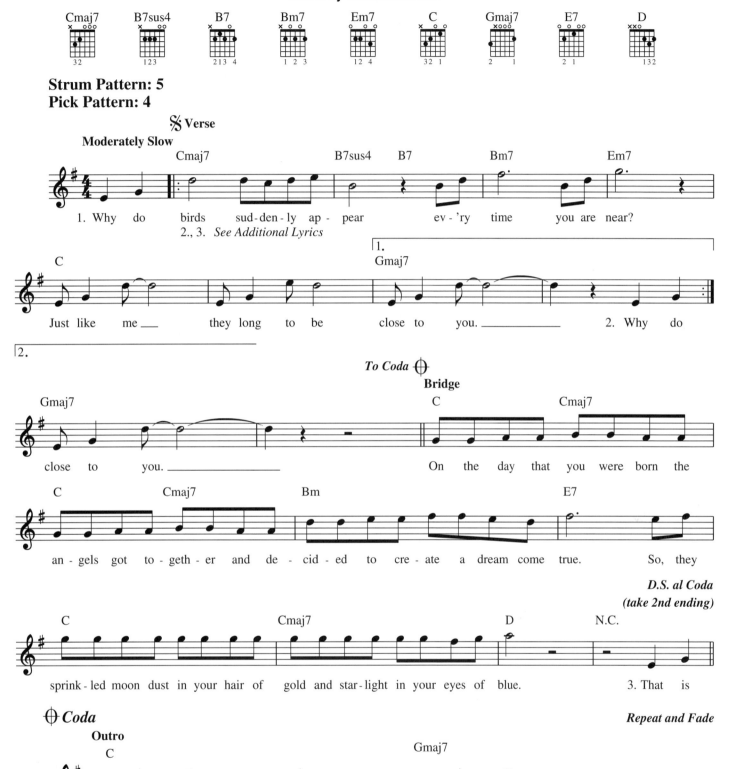

Strum Pattern: 5
Pick Pattern: 4

Additional Lyrics

2. Why do stars fall down from the sky
Ev'ry time you walk by?
Just like me they long to be
Close to you.

3. That is why all the {boys/girls} in town
Follow you all around.
Just like me they long to be
Close to you.

Beyond the Sea

English Lyrics by Jack Lawrence
Music and French Lyrics by Charles Trenet

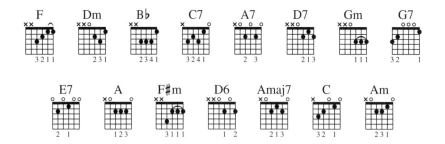

Verse
Moderately

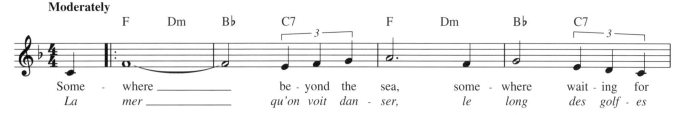

Some - where _____ be - yond the sea, some - where wait - ing for
La mer _____ *qu'on voit dan - ser, le long des golf - es*

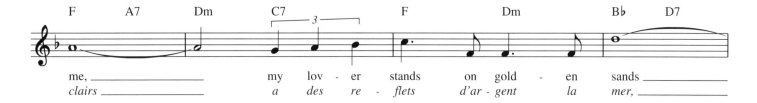

me, _____ my lov - er stands on gold - en sands _____
clairs _____ *a des re - flets d'ar - gent la mer,* _____

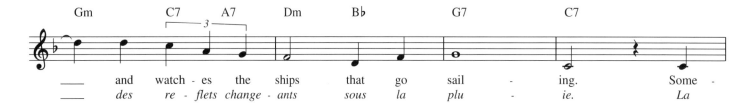

_____ and watch - es the ships that go sail - ing. Some -
_____ *des re - flets change - ants sous la plu - ie. La*

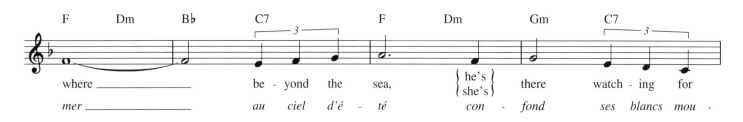

where _____ be - yond the sea, {he's} {she's} there watch - ing for
mer _____ *au ciel d'é - té con - fond ses blancs mou -*

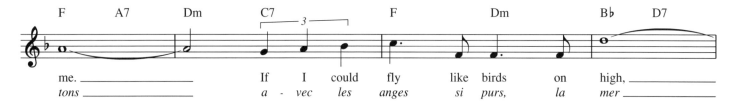

me. _____ If I could fly like birds on high, _____
tons _____ *a - vec les anges si purs, la mer* _____

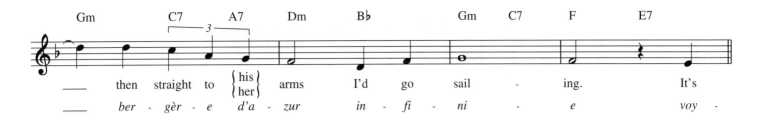

_____ then straight to {his / her} arms I'd go sail - ing. It's
_____ ber - gèr - e d'a - zur in - fi - ni - e voy -

Bridge

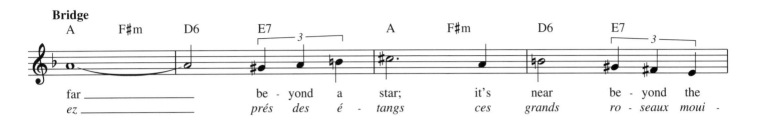

far _____ be - yond a star; it's near be - yond the
ez _____ prés des é - tangs ces grands ro - seaux moui -

moon. _____ I know _____ be - yond a
llés. _____ Voy - ez _____ ces oi - seaux

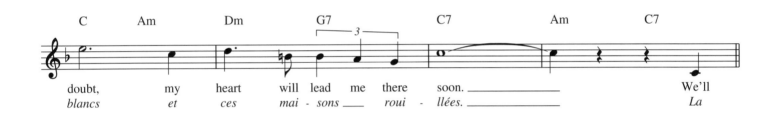

doubt, my heart will lead me there soon. _____ We'll
blancs et ces mai - sons _____ roui - llées. _____ La

Outro

meet _____ be - yond the shore; we'll kiss just as be - fore. _____
mer _____ les a ber - cés le long des golf - es clairs _____

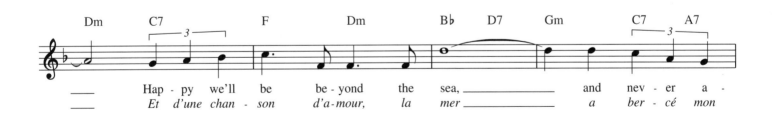

_____ Hap - py we'll be be - yond the sea, _____ and nev - er a -
_____ Et d'une chan - son d'a - mour, la mer _____ a ber - cé mon

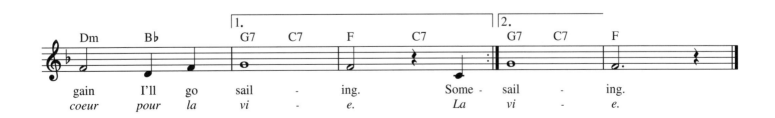

gain I'll go sail - ing. Some - sail - ing.
coeur pour la vi - e. La vi - e.

137

Come to My Window

Words and Music by Melissa Etheridge

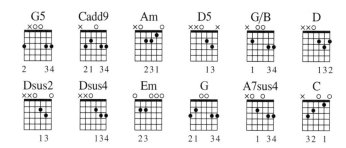

Intro
Moderately slow

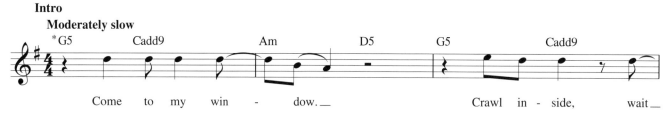

Come to my win - dow. ___ Crawl in - side, wait ___

* One strum per chord, next 6 meas.

___ by the light ___ of the moon. ___ Come ___ to my win - dow, ___ I'll be home

** Strum Pattern: 3
** Pick Pattern: 4
Faster

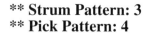

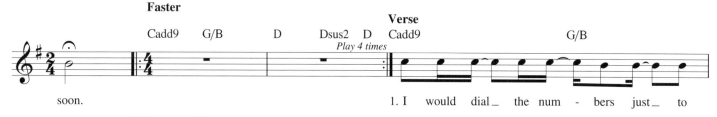

soon.   1. I would dial ___ the num - bers just ___ to

** Play patterns 2 times per measure.

lis - ten to ___ your breath. ___ And I would stand ___ in - side ___ my hell ___ and hold ___

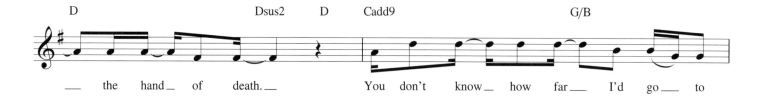

___ the hand ___ of death. ___ You don't know ___ how far ___ I'd go ___ to

Donna

Words and Music by Ritchie Valens

Strum Pattern: 8
Pick Pattern: 8

Intro
Moderately

Oh, Don - na, oh, Don - na, oh, Don - na, oh, Don - na.

Verse

1., 3. I had a girl, _____ Don - na _____ was her name, since she left me _____ I've
2. *See additional lyrics*

nev - er _____ been the same, _____ 'cause I love _____ my _____ girl, _____ Don - na, where _____ can you

To Coda

be, _____ where can _____ you be? Don - na, _____ where _ can you be, _____ where _ can you

Bridge

be? _____ Oh, dar - lin' _____ now that you're gone _____ I don't know what I'll _____

D.S. al Coda
(take 1st ending)

do. All _____ my smiles _____ and all my love for _____ you. _____

Coda
Outro

Repeat and fade

Oh, Don - na, oh, Don - na, oh, Don - na, oh, Don - na.

Additional Lyrics

2. Now that you're gone, I'm left all alone,
All by myself to wander and roam,
'Cause I love you girl,
Donna, where can you be,
Where can you be?

Heart Shaped Box

Words and Music by Kurt Cobain

Strum Pattern: 1, 3
Pick Pattern: 2, 4

Intro
Moderately

 Verse

1., 3. She ___ eyes me like ___ a Pi - sces when ___ I ___ am weak. ___
2. *See additional lyrics*

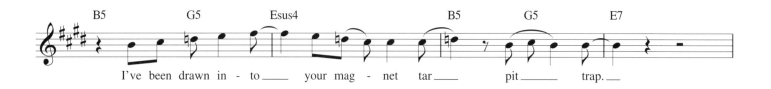

I've been locked in - side ___ your heart ___ shaped box ___ for ___ weeks. ___

I've been drawn in - to ___ your mag - net tar ___ pit ___ trap. ___

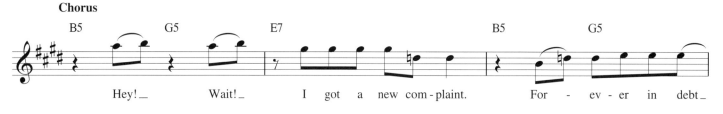

I wish I could eat ___ your can - cer when ___ you ___ turn black. ___

Chorus

Hey! ___ Wait! ___ I got a new com - plaint. For - ev - er in debt ___

___ to your price - less ad - vice. ___ Hey! ___ Wait! ___ I got a new com - plaint.

For - ev - er in debt___ to your price - less ad - vice.___ Hey! _ Wait!_

I got a new com - plaint. For - ev - er in debt___ to your price - less ad - vice.___

To Coda ⊕

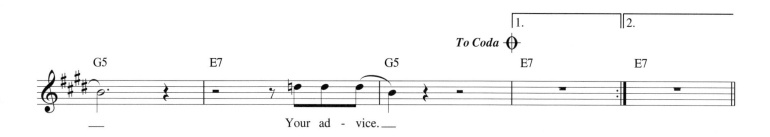

|1. |2.

___ Your ad - vice. ___

Guitar Solo

D.S. al Coda

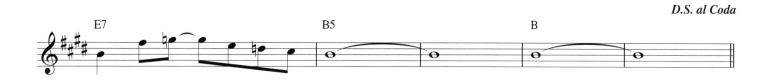

⊕ **Coda**

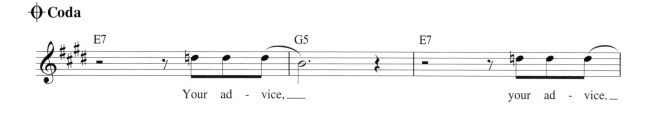

Your ad - vice,___ your ad - vice.___

___ *rit.*

Additional Lyrics

2. Meat eating orchids forgive no one just yet.
Cut myself on angel hair and baby's breath.
Broken hymen of your highness, I'm left black.
Throw down your umbilical noose so I can climb right back.

I Left My Heart in San Francisco

Words by Douglass Cross
Music by George Cory

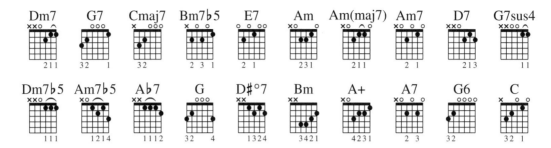

Strum Pattern: 8
Pick Pattern: 8

Intro
Moderately

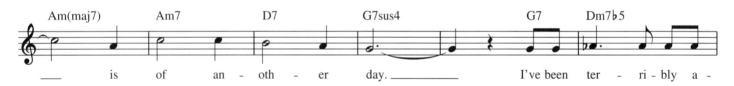

Strum Pattern: 4
Pick Pattern: 1

Chorus

it calls to me. To be where lit-tle ___ ca-ble cars ___

___ climb half-way ___ to the stars! ___ The morn-ing fog ___

___ may chill the air; I don't care! My love waits there

in San Fran-cis-co, ___ a-bove the blue ___

___ and wind-y sea. When I come home to

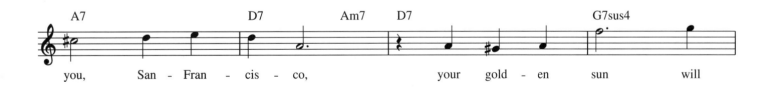

you, San-Fran-cis-co, your gold-en sun will

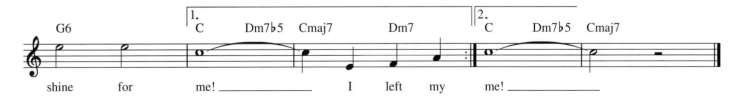

shine for me! ___ I left my me! ___

I've Got You Under My Skin

from BORN TO DANCE
Words and Music by Cole Porter

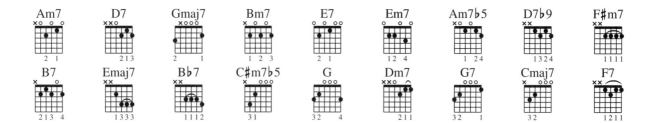

Strum Pattern: 3, 4
Pick Pattern: 3, 6

Verse
Moderately

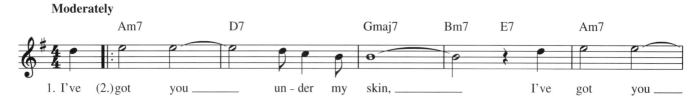

1. I've (2.)got you _____ un-der my skin, _____ I've got you _____

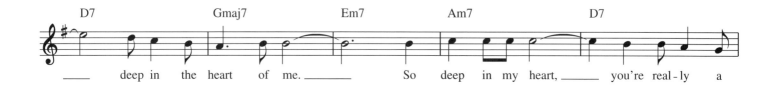

_____ deep in the heart of me. _____ So deep in my heart, _____ you're real-ly a

part of me. _____ I've got you _____ un-der my

skin. _____ I tried so _____ not to give in, _____ I

said to my-self, "this af-fair nev-er will go so well." _____ But why should I try to re-

sist when dar-ling, I know so well, _____ I've got you _____ un-der my

146

skin. _____ I'd sac-ri-fice an-y-thing, come what might, for the
sake of hav-ing you near, in spite of a warn-ing voice that comes in the night and re-
peats and re-peats in my ear: _____ "Don't you know, lit-tle fool, _____ you nev-er can win, _____
_____ use your men-tal-i-ty, _____ wake up to re-al-i-ty." _____ But each
time I do, just the thought of you makes me stop be-fore I be-gin, 'cause I've got you _____
_____ un-der my skin. _____ 2. I've skin.

Rocky Top

Words and Music by Boudleaux Bryant and Felice Bryant

Strum Pattern: 4
Pick Pattern: 5

1. Wish that I was
3. *See Additional Lyrics*

on ol' Rock-y Top down in the Tenn-es-see hills. Ain't no smog-gy smoke on Rock-y Top,

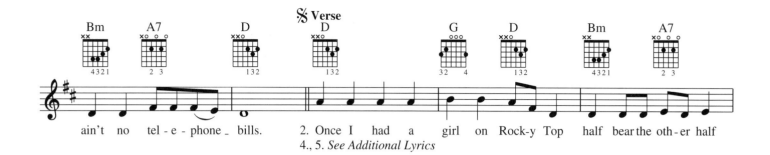

ain't no tel-e-phone bills. 2. Once I had a girl on Rock-y Top half bear the oth-er half

4., 5. *See Additional Lyrics*

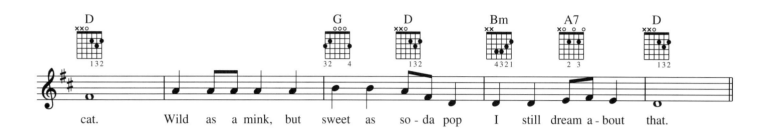

cat. Wild as a mink, but sweet as so-da pop I still dream a-bout that.

Chorus

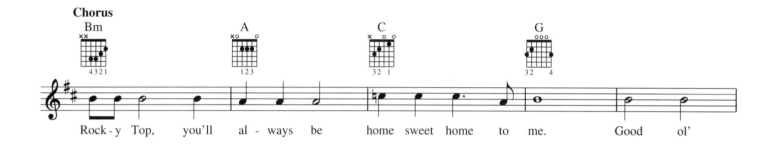

Rock-y Top, you'll al-ways be home sweet home to me. Good ol'

To Coda ⊕ | 1. | | 2. *D.S. al Coda*

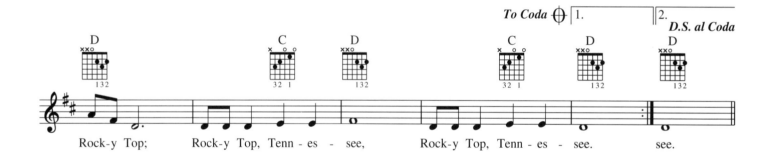

Rock-y Top; Rock-y Top, Tenn-es - see, Rock-y Top, Tenn-es - see. see.

⊕ *Coda*

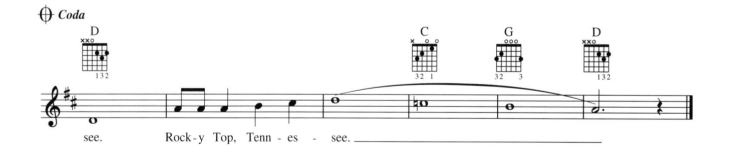

see. Rock-y Top, Tenn-es - see. ____

Additional Lyrics

3. Once two strangers climbed ol' Rocky Top, lookin' for a moonshine still.
Strangers ain't come down from Rocky Top, reckon they never will.

4. Corn won't grow at all on Rocky Top, dirt's too rocky by far.
That's why all the folks on Rocky Top get their corn from a jar.

5. I've had years of cramped-up city life, trapped like a duck in a pen.
All I know is it's a pity life can't be simple again.

In a Sentimental Mood

Words and Music by Duke Ellington, Irving Mills and Manny Kurtz

It's My Party

Words and Music by Herb Wiener, Wally Gold and John Gluck, Jr.

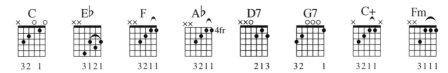

Strum Pattern: 3, 6
Pick Pattern: 4, 5

Verse
Moderately bright

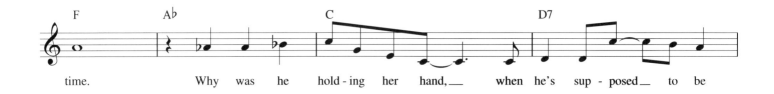

1. No-bod-y knows where my John-ny has gone, but Ju-dy left the same
2., 3. *See additional lyrics*

time. Why was he hold-ing her hand, when he's sup-posed to be

Chorus

mine? It's my par-ty, and I'll cry if I want to,

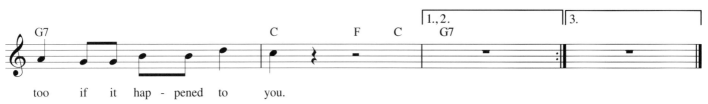

cry if I want to, cry if I want to. You would cry

too if it hap-pened to you.

Additional Lyrics

2. Play all my records; keep dancing all night,
   But leave alone for awhile.
   'Til Johnny's dancing with me,
   I've got no reason to smile.

3. Judy and Johnny just walked through the door,
   Like a queen with her king.
   Oh, what a birthday surprise,
   Judy's wearing his ring.

Sway
(Quien será)

English Words by Norman Gimbel
Spanish Words and Music by Pablo Beltran Ruiz

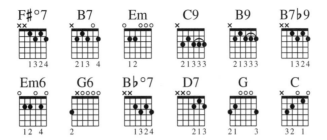

Strum Pattern: 3, 4
Pick Pattern: 1, 3

Verse

Moderately

When ma-rim-ba rhy-thms start to play, dance with me, make me sway.

Like the la-zy o-cean hugs the shore, hold me close, sway me more.

Like a flow-er bend-ing in the breeze, bend with me, sway with ease.

When we dance you have a way with me, stay with me, sway with me.

Bridge

Oth-er dan-cers may be on the floor, dear, but my eyes will see on-ly you.

On-ly you have that ma-gic tech-nique, when we sway I grow weak.

Outro

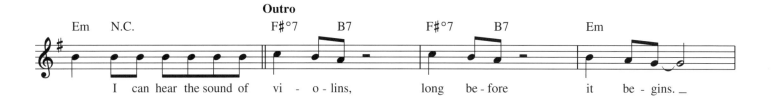

I can hear the sound of vi - o - lins, long be - fore it be - gins. _

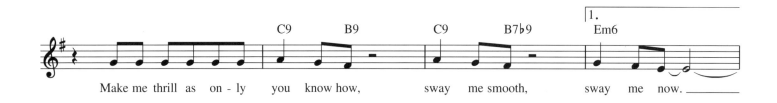

Make me thrill as on - ly you know how, sway me smooth, sway me now. _____

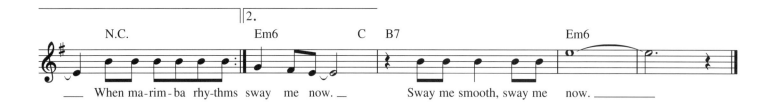

_ When ma - rim - ba rhy - thms sway me now. _ Sway me smooth, sway me now. _____

You Are the Sunshine of My Life

Words and Music by Stevie Wonder

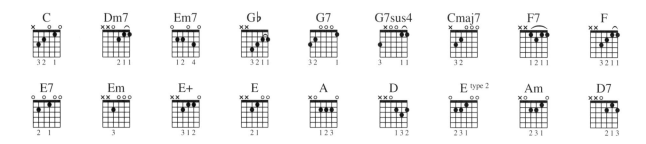

Strum Pattern: 5
Pick Pattern: 4

Chorus
Moderately

You are the sun - shine of __ my life, __

that's why I'll al - ways { be __ / stay __ } a - round. _____

You are the ap - ple of ___ my eye. ___

For - ev - er you'll ___ stay in ___ my heart. _____

Verse

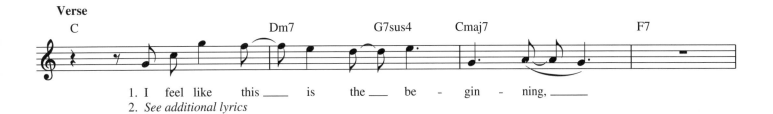

1. I feel like this ___ is the ___ be - gin - ning, _____
2. *See additional lyrics*

'though I've loved you ___ for a mil - lion years. ___

And if I thought ___ our love ___ was _____ end - ing, _____

I'd ___ find ___ my - self ___ drown - ing in my ___ own

1.   **2.**

D.C. and fade

tears.   { Whoa, _____ whoa.   { Whoa. ___ _____

Additional Lyrics

2. You must have known that I was lonely.
   Because you came to my rescue.
   And I know that this must be heaven;
   How could so much love be inside of you?

Limbo Rock

Words and Music by Billy Strange and Jon Sheldon

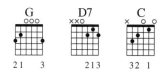

Strum Pattern: 4, 3
Pick Pattern: 6, 3

Intro
Moderate Latin Rock

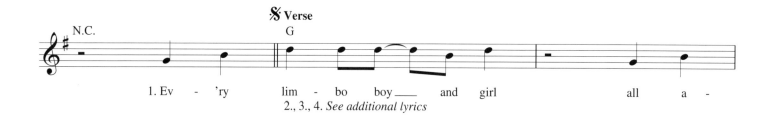

1. Ev - 'ry lim - bo boy___ and girl all a-

2., 3., 4. See additional lyrics

round the lim - bo world, gon - na do the Lim - bo Rock

all a - round the lim - bo clock. Jack be

Chorus

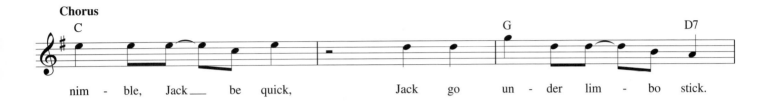

nim - ble, Jack __ be quick, Jack go un - der lim - bo stick.

To Coda 1

To Coda 2

Fine

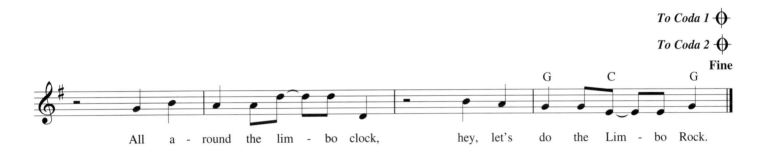

All a - round the lim - bo clock, hey, let's do the Lim - bo Rock.

Breakdown

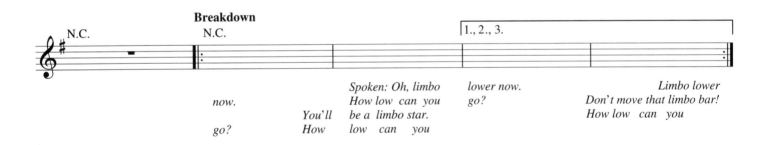

now.

go?

Spoken: Oh, limbo

How low can you

You'll be a limbo star.

How low can you

lower now.

go?

Limbo lower

Don't move that limbo bar!

How low can you

go?

2. First you

Coda 1

3. La, la

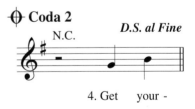

Coda 2

4. Get your -

Additional lyrics

2. First you spread your limbo feet,
Then you move to limbo beat.
Limbo ankle, limbo knee;
Bend back, like the limbo tree.

3. La, la, la, la, la, la, la... etc.
(cont. through Chorus)

4. Get yourself a limbo girl,
Give that chick a limbo whirl.
There's a limbo moon above,
You will fall in limbo love.

The Loco-Motion

Words and Music by Gerry Goffin and Carole King

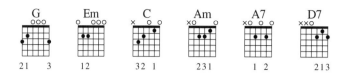

Strum Pattern: 3, 4
Pick Pattern: 6

Intro
Brightly

1. Ev - 'ry - bod - y's do - in' a

brand new dance ___ now. (C'm on ba - by, do ___ the Lo - co - mo - tion.) I

know you'll get to like it if you give it a chance ___ now. (C'm on ba - by, do ___

___ the Lo - co - mo - tion.) My lit - tle ba - by sis - ter can do it with ease. ___ It's

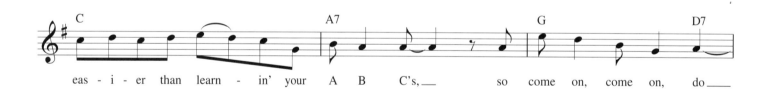

eas - i - er than learn - in' your A B C's, ___ so come on, come on, do ___

___ the Lo - co - mo - tion with me. You got - ta swing your hips now.

Bridge

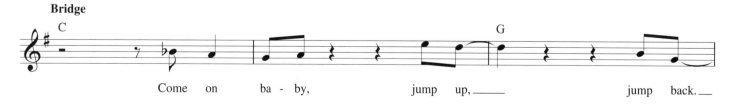

Come on ba - by, jump up, ___ jump back. ___

_____ Oh, well, I think you got the knack.

Verse

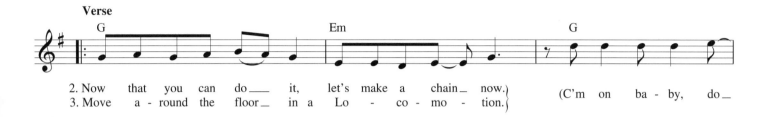
2. Now that you can do ___ it, let's make a chain ___ now.)
3. Move a - round the floor ___ in a Lo - co - mo - tion.) (C'm on ba - by, do ___

___ the Lo - co - mo - tion.) A chug - a - chug - a mo - tion like a rail - road train ___ now.)
Do it hold - in' hands ___ if ___ you get the no - tion.)

(C'm on ba - by, do ___ the Lo - co - mo - tion.) Do it nice and eas - y now, ___
There's nev - er been a dance ___ that's so

don't lose con - trol. ___ A lit - tle bit of rhy - thm and a lot of soul. ___
eas - y to do. ___ It'll e - ven make you hap - py when you're feel - in' blue. ___ So,

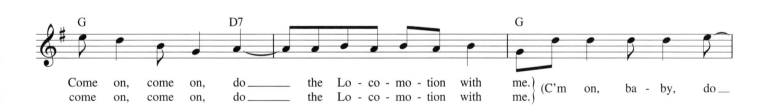
Come on, come on, do ___ the Lo - co - mo - tion with me.) (C'm on, ba - by, do ___
come on, come on, do ___ the Lo - co - mo - tion with me.)

Outro   *Repeat and fade*

___ the Lo - co - mo - tion.)   (C'm on, ba - by, do ___ the Lo - co - mo - tion.)

Save the Last Dance for Me

Words and Music by Doc Pomus and Mort Shuman

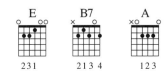

Strum Pattern: 2
Pick Pattern: 4

1. You can dance ev - 'ry dance with the guy who gives
2., 3. *See additional lyrics*

___ you the eye; let him hold you tight. ___ You can

smile ___ ev - 'ry smile for the man who held ___ your hand ___ 'neath the

pale moon - light. ___ { 1., 2. But 3. 'Cause } don't for - get who's tak - ing you home ___

___ and in whose arms you're gon - na be. So dar - lin', save the

last dance ___ for ___ me. Mm. ___ 2. Oh, I me. Mm.

Bridge

1. Ba - by, don't you know I love you so?__ Can't you feel it when we
2. *Instrumental*

touch? I will nev - er, nev - er let you go.__

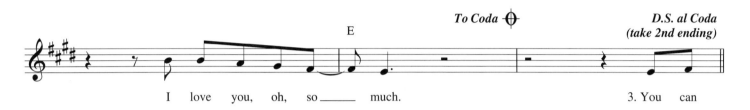

To Coda ⊕   *D.S. al Coda (take 2nd ending)*

I love you, oh, so ____ much. 3. You can

⊕ **Coda** **Chorus**

'Cause don't for - get who's tak - ing you home ____ and in whose arms you're

gon - na be. So, dar - lin', save the

last dance ____ for ____ me. Mm. ____

Outro

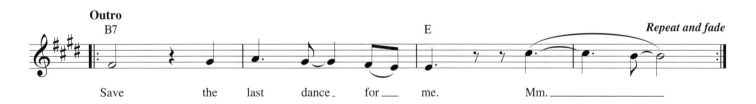

Repeat and fade

Save the last dance__ for __ me. Mm. ____

Additional Lyrics

2. Oh, I know that the music's fine
Like sparkling wine; go and have your fun.
Laugh and sing, but while we're apart
Don't give your heart to anyone.

3. You can dance, go and carry on
Till the night is gone and it's time to go.
If he asks if you're all alone,
Can he take you home, you must tell him no.

Tico Tico
(Tico no fuba)

Words and Music by Zequinha Abreu, Aloysio Oliveira and Ervin Drake

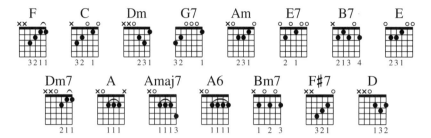

Strum Pattern: 1, 3
Pick Pattern: 2, 4

Intro
Bright Samba

Oh, ti - co -
O ti - co -

Verse

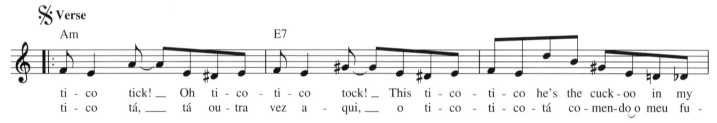

ti - co tick!__ Oh ti - co - ti - co tock!__ This ti - co - ti - co he's the cuck - oo in my
ti - co tá,__ tá ou - tra vez a - qui,__ o ti - co - ti - co - tá co - men - do o meu fu -

clock. And when he says: "Cuck - oo!"__ he means it's time to woo;__ it's "Ti - co
bá: Si o ti - co - ti - co tem,__ tem que se a - li - men - tar,__ Que vá co -

time" for all the lov - ers in the block. I've got a heav - y date __ a tête - a -
mer u - mas mi - nho - cas no po - mar. O ti - co - ti - co tá __ tá ou - tra

tête at eight, _ so speak, oh ti - co, tell me is it get - ting latc? If I'm on
vez a - qui, __ o ti - co - ti - co tá co - men - do o meu fu - bá. Eu sei que

time: "Cuck - oo!" __ but if I'm late, "Woo - woo!" __ The one my heart has gone to may not want to
el - le vem vi - ver no meu quin - tal, __ e vem com a - res de ca - ña - rio e de par -

wait! For just a bir - die, and a bir - die who goes no - where, he knows of
dal. Mas por fa - vor ti - ra es - se bi - cho fo ce - lei - ro, por que el-le a -

ev - 'ry Lov - ers' Lane and how to go there; for in af - fairs of the heart, __ my ti - co's
ca - ba co - men-do o fu - bá in - tei - ro. Ti - ra es - se ti - co de lá, ___ de ci - ma

ter - ri - bly smart, __ he tells me: "Gen - tly, sen - ti - ment - 'ly at the start!" Oh, oh, I
do meu fu - bá. ___ Tem tan - ta fru - ta que el - le po - de pi - ni - car. Eu já fiz

hear my lit - tle ti - co - ti - co call - ing, be - cause the time is right and shades of night are
tu - do pa - ra ver se con - se - gui - a. Bo - tei al - pis - te pa - ra ver si el - le co -

fall - ing. I love that not - so - cuck - oo cuck - oo in the clock: ti - co -
mi - a. Bo - tei um ga - to um es - pan - to - lho e um al - ça - pão, mas el - le a - cha que o fu -

To Coda | 1. | 2. | **Interlude**

ti - co - ti - co ti - co - ti - co tock. Oh, ti - co tock.
bá é que é bo - a a - li - men - ta - ção. O ti - co ção.

D.S. al Coda   **Coda**

Oh, ti - co tock. ___
O ti - co ção. ___

Wheel in the Sky

Words and Music by Robert Fleischman, Neal Schon and Diane Valory

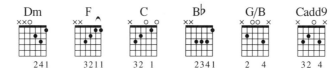

Strum Pattern: 3, 4
Pick Pattern: 4, 5

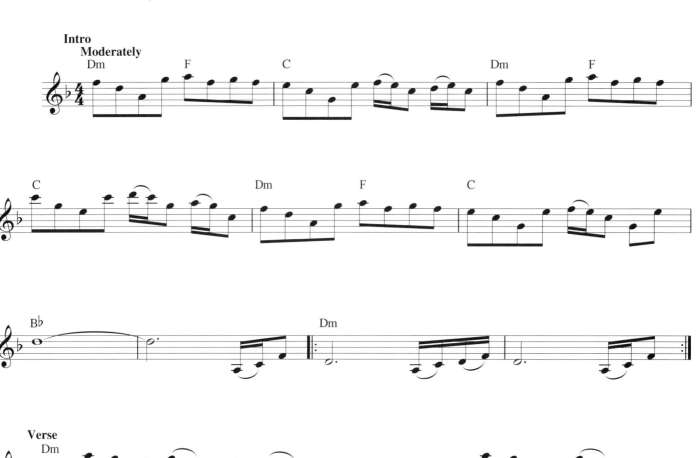

1. Win - ter is here __ a - gain, __ oh Lord. Have-n't been home __ in a
2. *See additional lyrics*

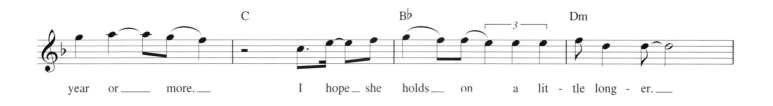

year or __ more. __ I hope __ she holds __ on a lit - tle long - er. __

Sent a let - ter on a long __ sum - mer day made of sil - ver,

don't know,_ I don't_ know._____ Oh, the

Outro-Chorus

wheel in the sky_ keeps on turn - in'.___ Oo, I don't know_ where I'll be to - mor - row.____

Wheel in the sky_ keeps on turn - in'.___ Oo, I don't know,_ I don't know,_ I don't_ know.____

Wheel in the sky__ keeps on turn - in'. Don't know where I'll be to -

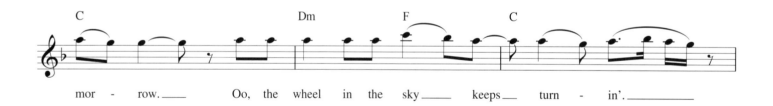

mor - row.____ Oo, the wheel in the sky___ keeps__ turn - in'._____

Repeat and fade

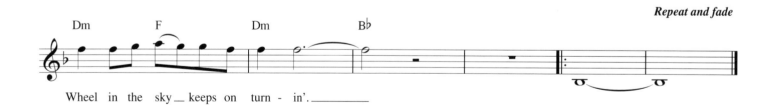

Wheel in the sky_ keeps on turn - in'._____

Additional Lyrics

2. I've been tryin' to make it home.
   Got to make it before too long.
   Oo, I can't take this very much longer, no.
   I'm stranded in the sleet and rain.
   Don't think I'm ever gonna make it home again.
   The mornin' sun is risin',
   It's kissin' the day.

You'll Be in My Heart
(Pop Version)

from Walt Disney Pictures' TARZAN ™
Words and Music by Phil Collins

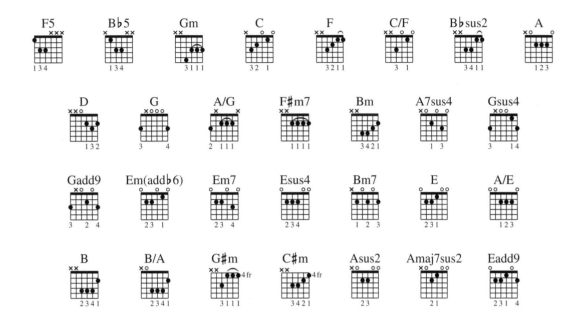

Strum Pattern: 2
Pick Pattern: 4

Intro

Moderately

Come stop your cry - ing; _ it will be all right. Just take my hand,

hold it tight. ___ I will pro - tect you from all a - round _ you.

%% Verse

I will be here; don't you _ cry.
1. For one so small you
2. *See additional lyrics*

seem so _ strong. _ My arms will hold you _ keep you safe and _ warm. _

this day on, ___ now ___ and for - ev - er - more. ___

You'll be in _____ my _ heart no mat-ter what _ they _ say. You'll
(You'll be here _ in my heart.)   (I'll be with you.)

be here in _____ my _ heart (I'll be there.) al - ways. Al -

ways _____ I'll be with you. I'll be

there for _ you al - ways, al - ways, _ and al - ways. ___

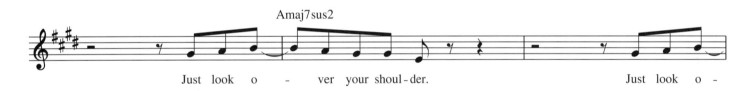

Just look o - ver your shoul - der. Just look o -

- ver your shoul - der. Just look o - ver your shoul - der;

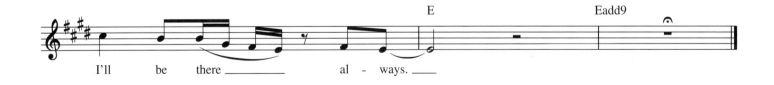

I'll be there _____ al - ways. ___

Additional Lyrics

2. Why can't they understand the way we feel?
They just don't trust what they can't explain.
I know we're diff'rent, but deep inside us
We're not that different at all.
And you'll be in my heart,...

Bridge When destiny calls you
You must be strong. (Gotta be strong.)
It may not be with you,
But you've got to hold on.
They'll see in time, I know.

Your Mama Don't Dance

Words and Music by Jim Messina and Kenny Loggins

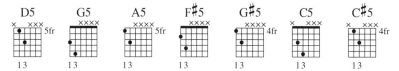

Strum Pattern: 1, 2

Your ma - ma don't dance and your

dad - dy don't rock and roll.___ Your ma - ma don't dance and your

dad - dy don't rock and roll.___ But when eve - nin' rolls a - round and it's

time to hit the town, where do you go? You got - ta rock it! The

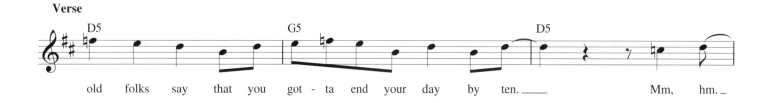

old folks say that you got - ta end your day by ten.___ Mm, hm.___

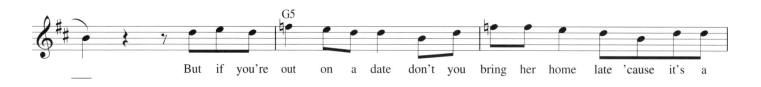

But if you're out on a date don't you bring her home late 'cause it's a

D5   A5

sin.   You know___ there's no ex - cuse, you know_

G5   D5

___ you're gon - na lose_ you nev - er win, ___   I'll say it a - gain. (And it's all be - cause...) Your

𝄋 Chorus

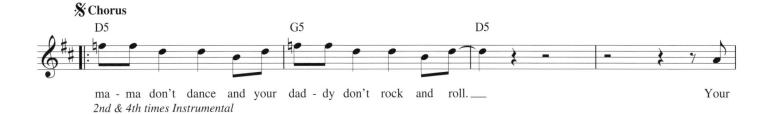

D5   G5   D5

ma - ma don't dance and your dad - dy don't rock and roll. __   Your
2nd & 4th times Instrumental

G5   D5

ma - ma don't dance and your dad - dy don't rock and roll. __   When

4th time, To Coda 🜖 | 1.

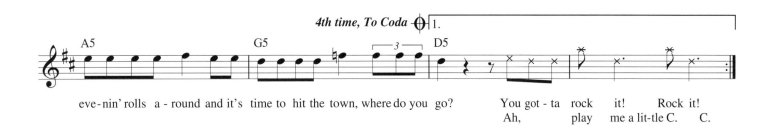

A5   G5   D5

eve - nin' rolls a - round and it's time to hit the town, where do you go?   You got - ta rock it!   Rock it!
Ah,   play me a lit-tle C.   C.

| 2.

Bridge

D5   F#5 G5   F#5 G5   F#5 G5   F#5

Spoken: Yeah, I pull into a drive-in and I found a place to park, we hoped into the back seat

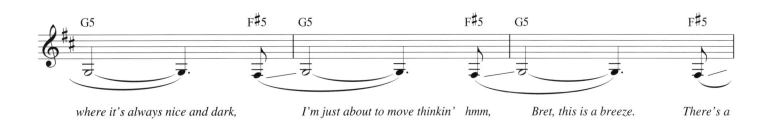

G5   F#5 G5   F#5 G5   F#5

where it's always nice and dark,   *I'm just about to move thinkin' hmm,*   *Bret, this is a breeze.*   *There's a*

light in my eye and a guy says, "Out of the car, long-hair." But ooh - wee,___ "You're com - in' with

D.S. al Coda
(take repeat)

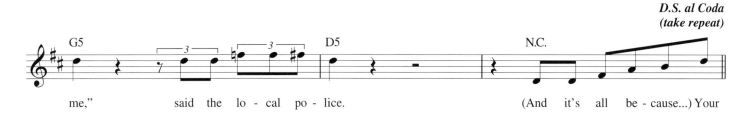

me," said the lo - cal po - lice. (And it's all be - cause...) Your

⊕ Coda

Outro

Your ma - ma don't dance and your dad - dy don't rock and roll.___
(Your

* One strum per chord, next 8 measures

___ It just ain't cool and you ain't a - bout to stop. Your
ma - ma don't dance and your dad - dy don't rock and roll.)

ma - ma don't dance and your dad - dy don't rock. Your ma - ma don't dance, no.___

___ She just don't dance, no.___ Your ma - ma don't dance and your

dad - dy don't rock and roll.___ Ah, yeah.___

A Day in the Life of a Fool
(Manha de carnaval)

Words by Carl Sigman
Music by Luiz Bonfa

Verse
Moderately

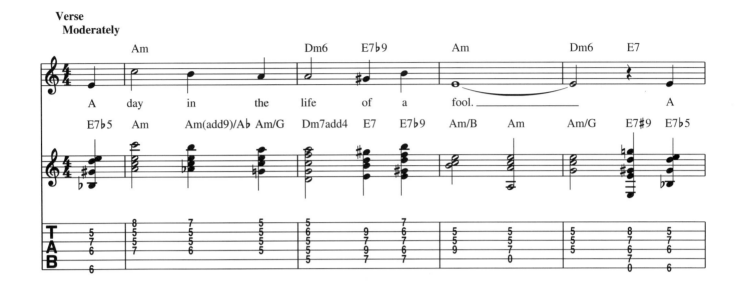

A day in the life of a fool. _____ A

sad and a long, lone-ly day. _____ I walk the

av-e-nue _____ and hope I'll run in-to _____ the wel-come

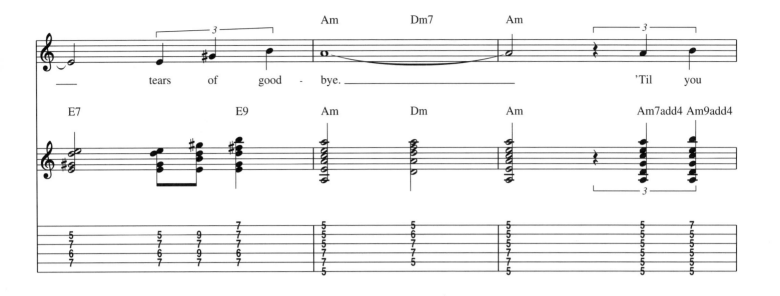

tears of good - bye. _____ 'Til you

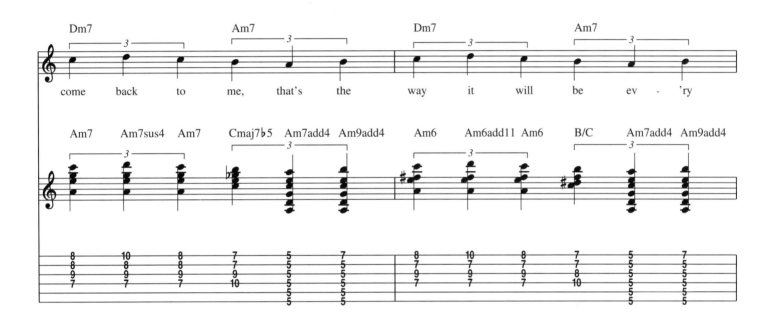

come back to me, that's the way it will be ev - 'ry

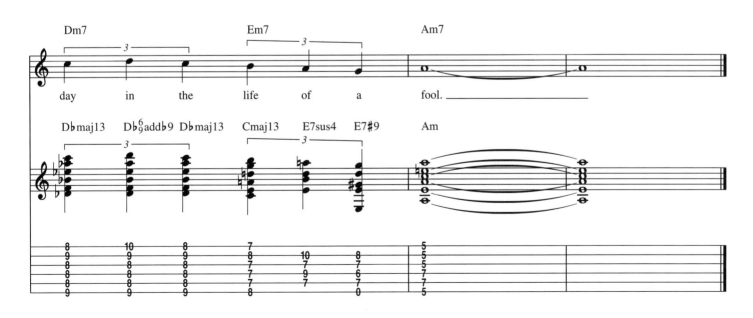

day in the life of a fool. _____

Easy to Love
(You'd Be So Easy to Love)

from BORN TO DANCE

Words and Music by Cole Porter

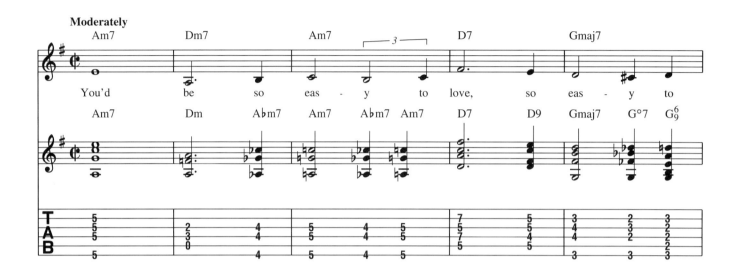

You'd be so eas-y to love, so eas-y to

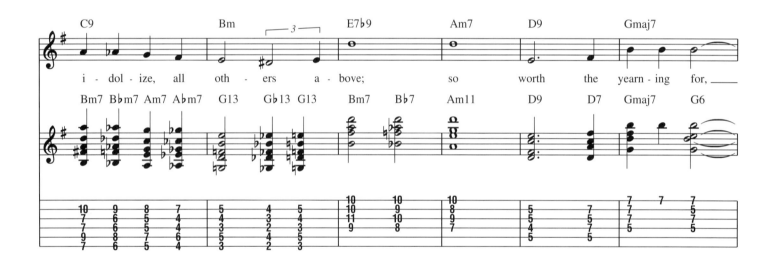

i-dol-ize, all oth-ers a-bove; so worth the yearn-ing for,

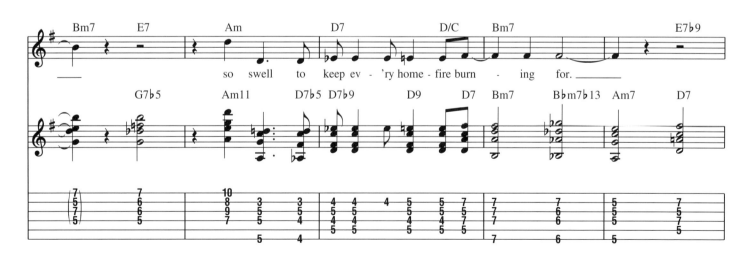

so swell to keep ev-'ry home-fire burn-ing for.

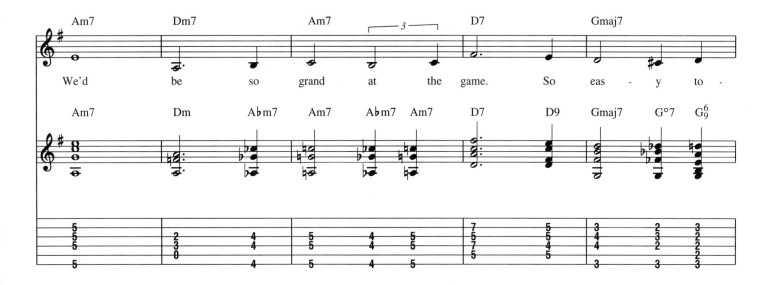

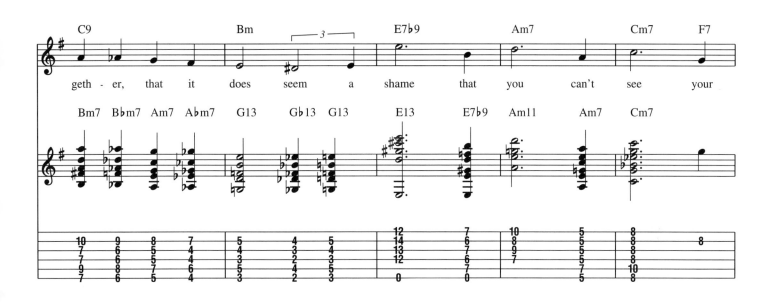

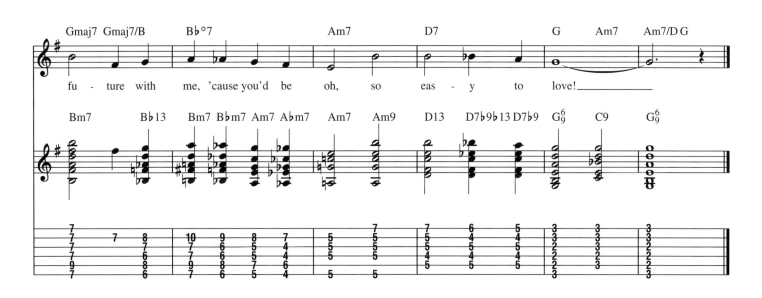

Falling in Love With Love

from THE BOYS FROM SYRACUSE

Words by Lorenz Hart
Music by Richard Rodgers

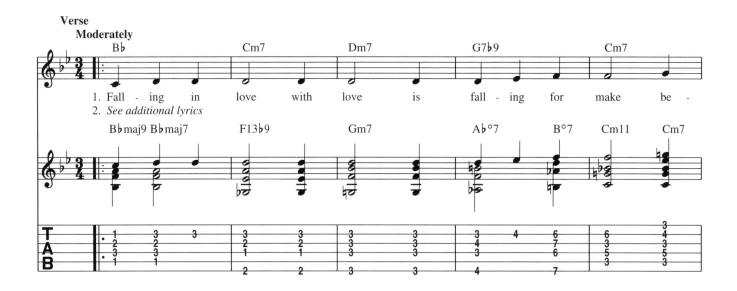

1. Fall - ing in love with love is fall - ing for make be -
2. *See additional lyrics*

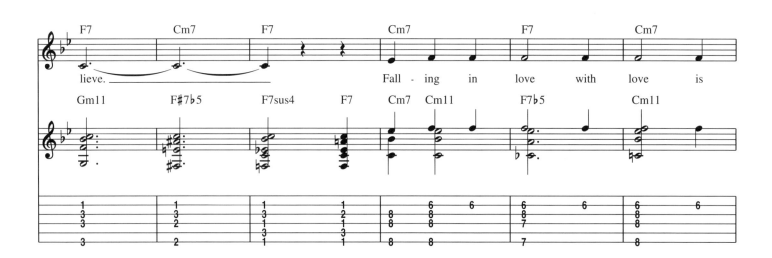

lieve. _____ Fall - ing in love with love is

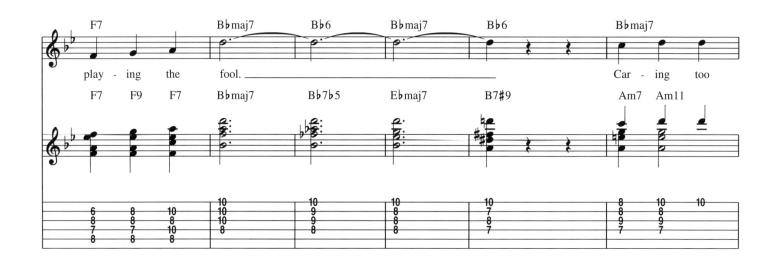

play - ing the fool. _____ Car - ing too

Moonlight in Vermont

Words and Music by John Blackburn and Karl Suessdorf

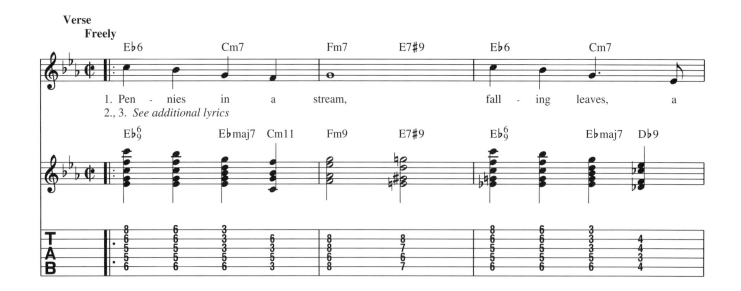

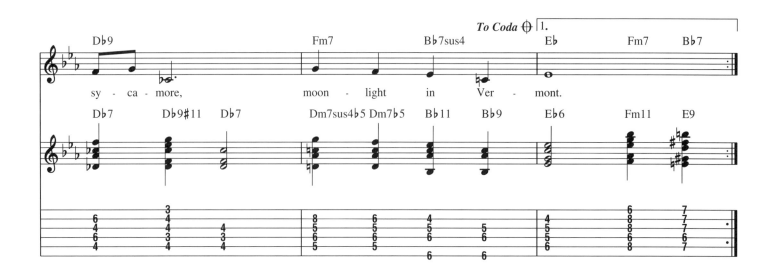

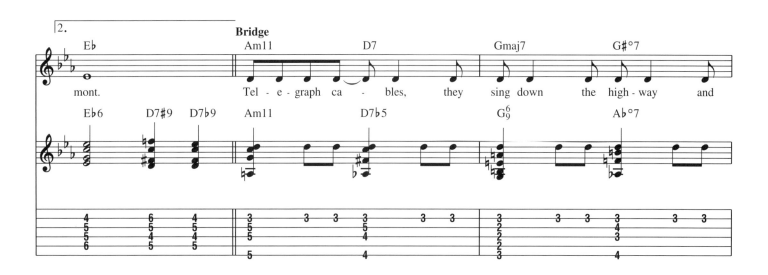

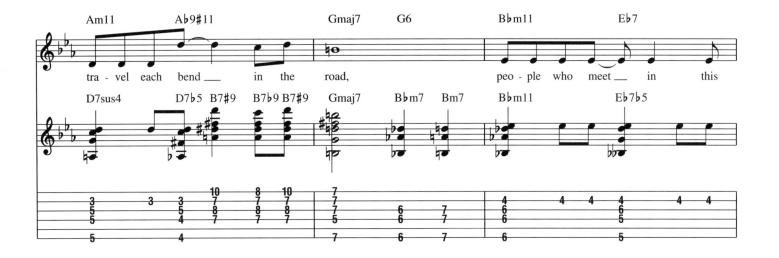

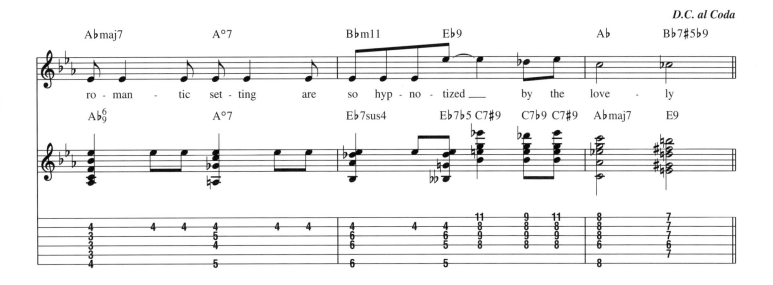

My Foolish Heart

from MY FOOLISH HEART
Words by Ned Washington
Music by Victor Young

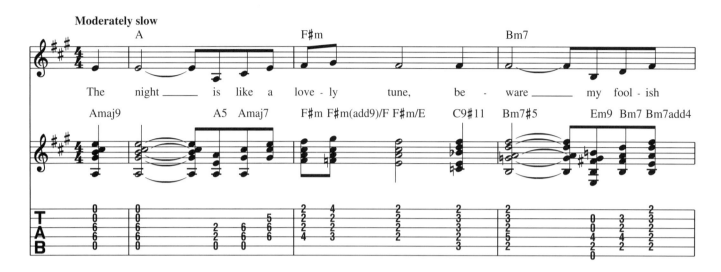

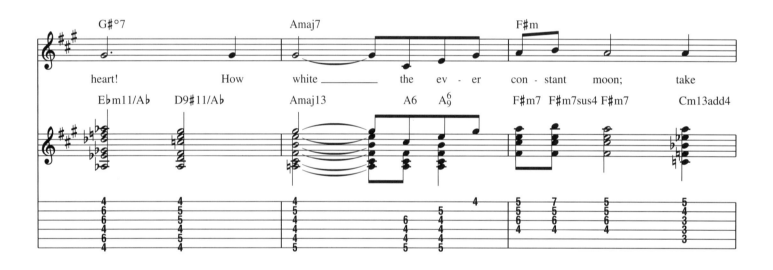

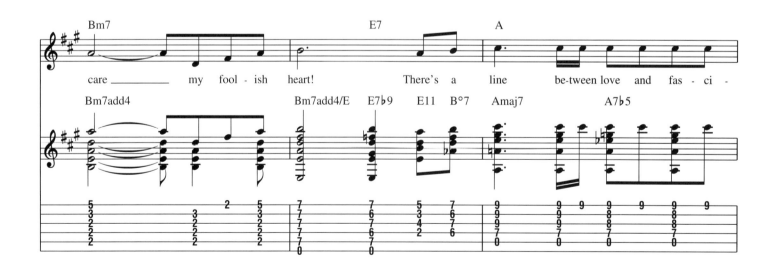

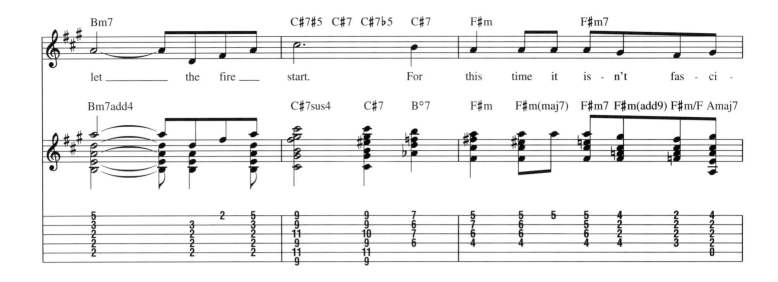

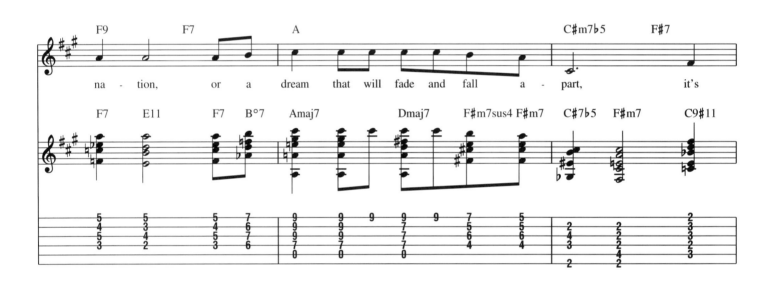

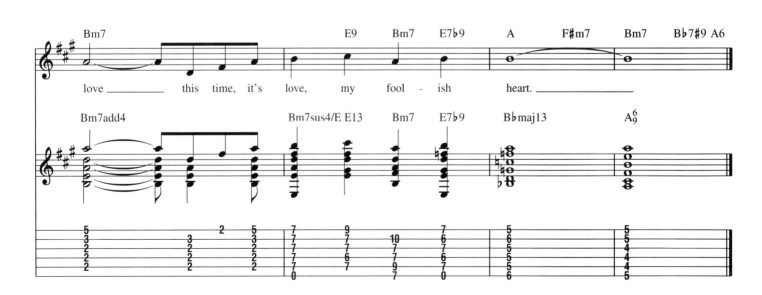

Bist du bei mir
(You Are With Me)

By Johann Sebastian Bach

Asturias (Prelude)

from CANTOS DE ESPAÑA, OP. 232

By Isaac Albéniz

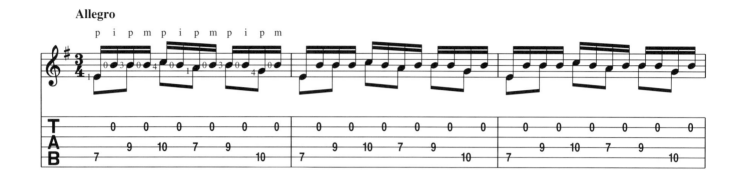

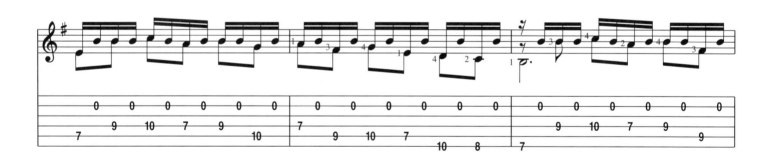

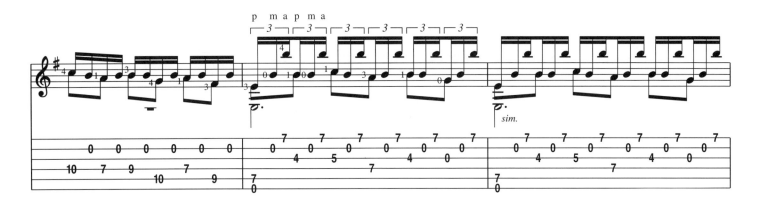

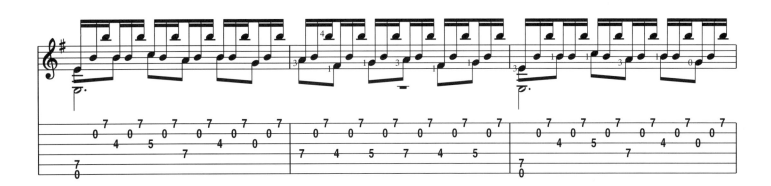

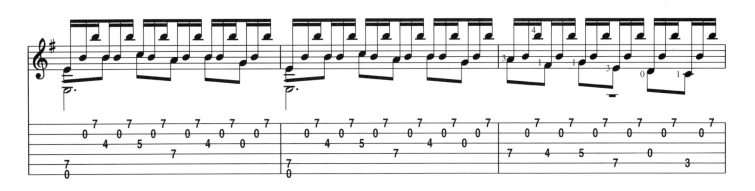

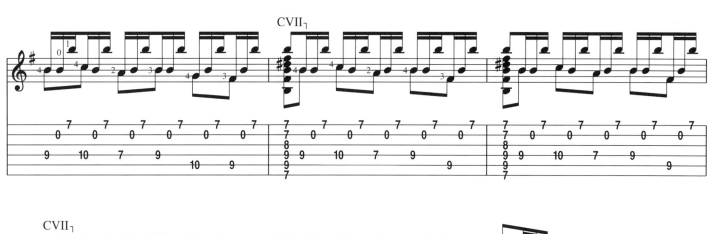

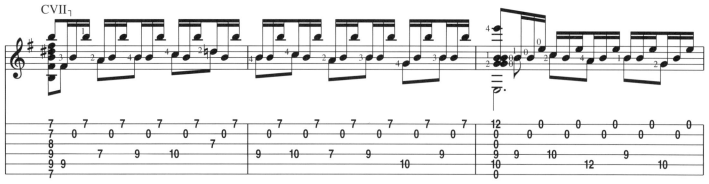

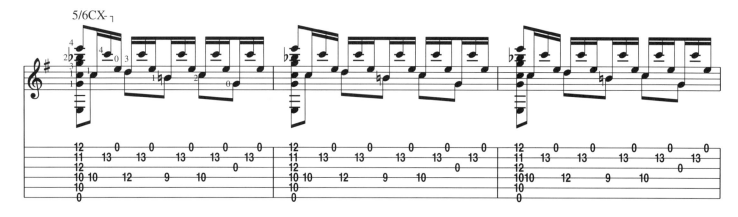

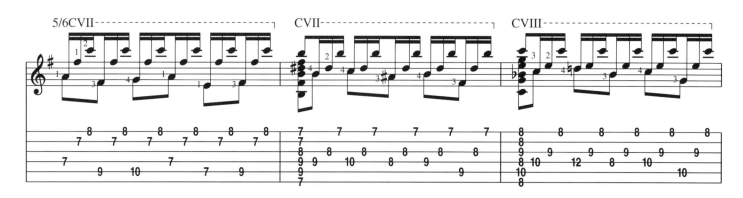

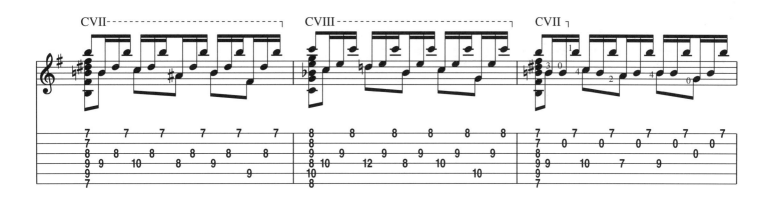

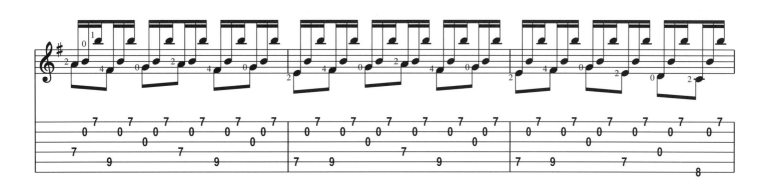

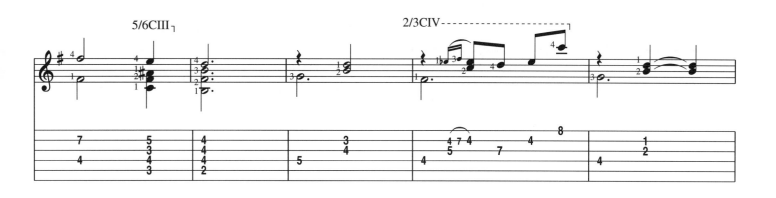

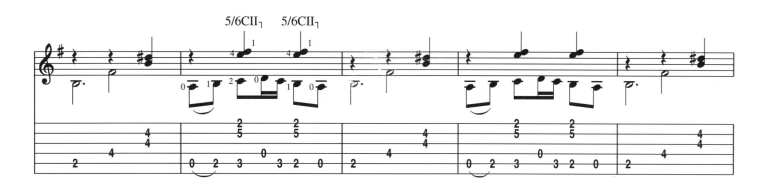

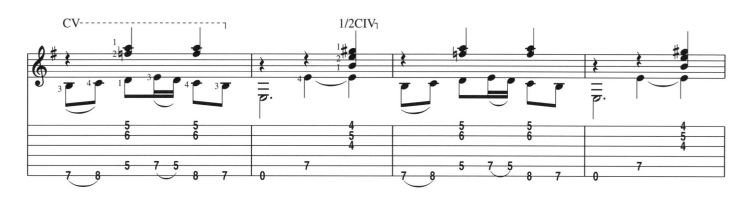

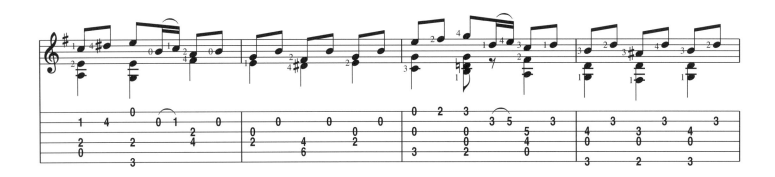

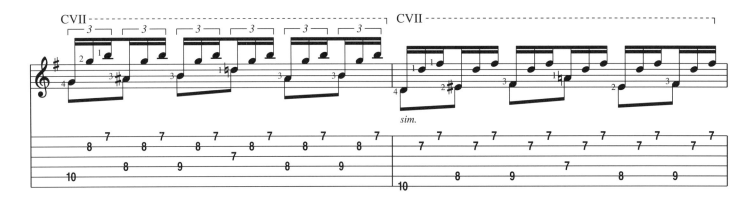

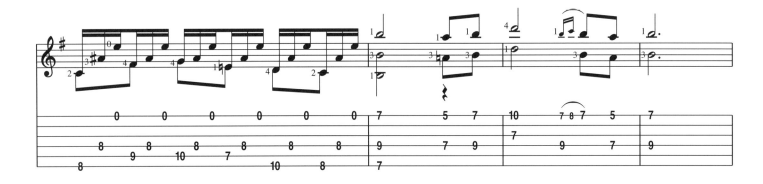

D.C. al Coda

⊕ Coda

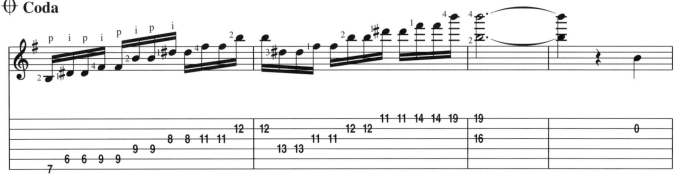

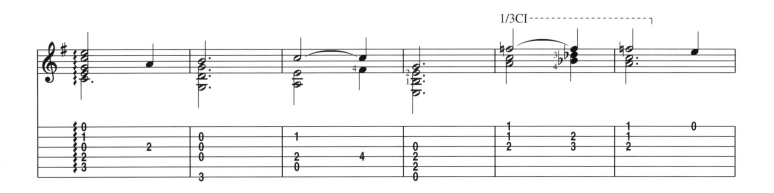

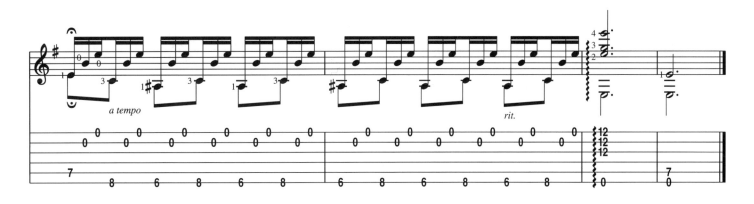

Study
Op. 6, No. 11

By Fernando Sor

Theme and Variations

on FOLIES d'ESPAGNE, OP. 45

By Mauro Giuliani

Theme

Andantino

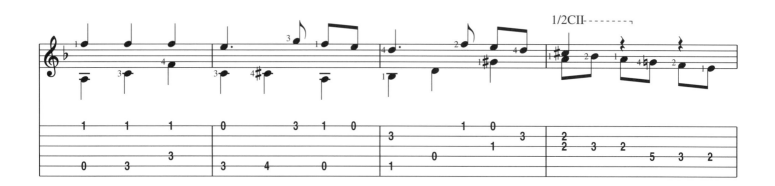

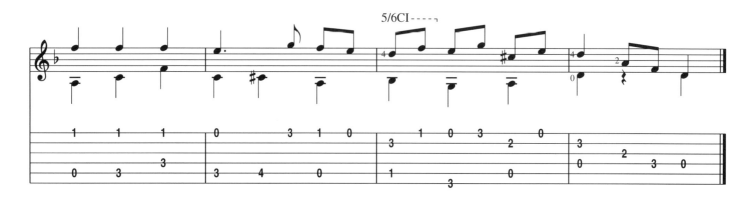

Variation 1

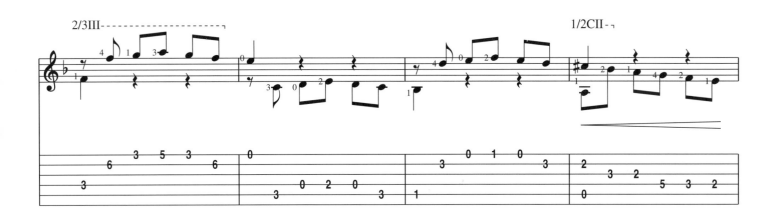

Variation 2

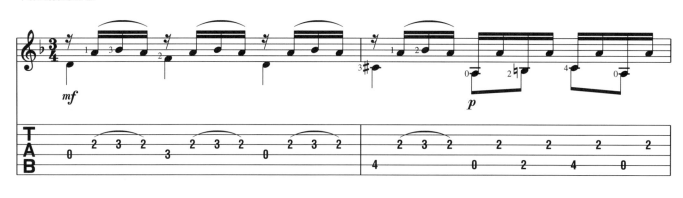

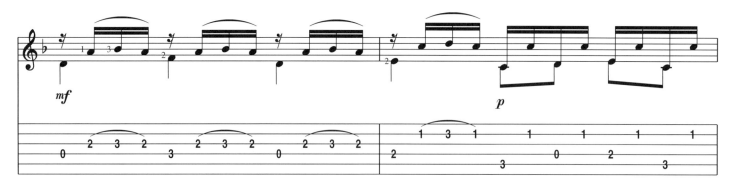

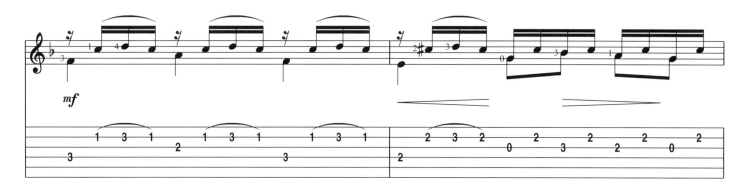

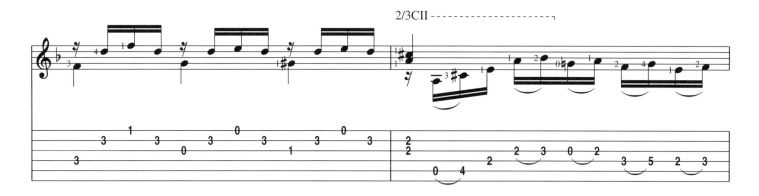

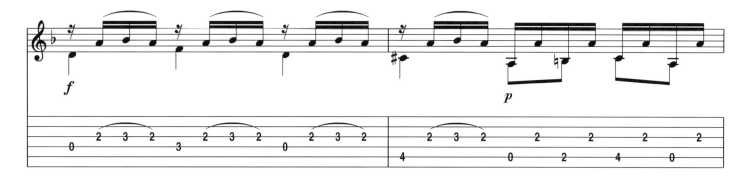

Variation 3

Variation 4

Variation 5

un poco piú Adagio

Variation 6

Allegro Vivace

Las folias de España

By Gaspar Sanz

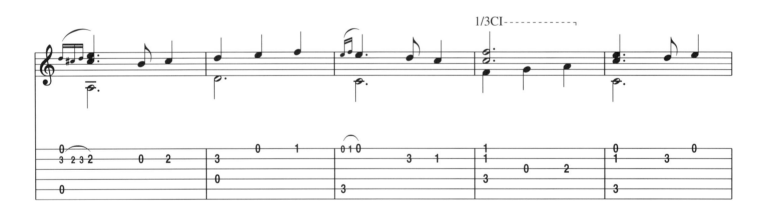

Crying

Words and Music by Roy Orbison and Joe Melson

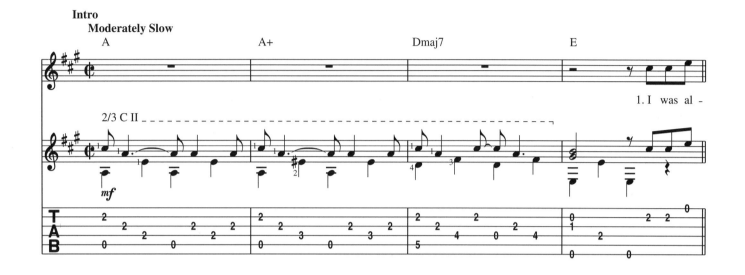

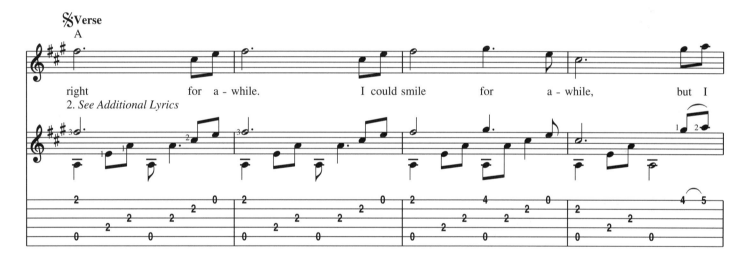

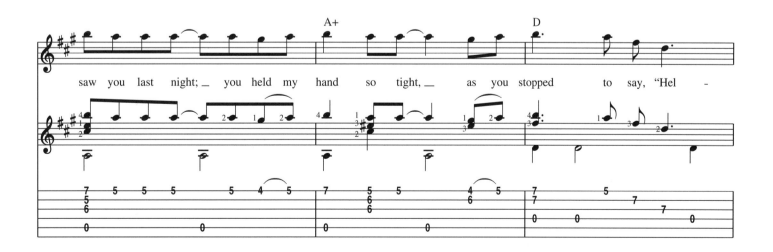

D.S. al Coda

✠ *Coda*

Additional Lyrics

2. I thought that I was over you,
   But it's true, so true,
   I love you even more than I did before,
   But darling, what can I do?
   For you don't love me and I'll always be…

Chorus Crying over you, crying over you.
   Yes, now you're gone and from this moment on
   I'll be crying, crying, crying, crying.
   Yeah, crying, crying over you.

Can't Help Falling in Love

from the Paramount Picture BLUE HAWAII

Words and Music by George David Weiss, Hugo Peretti and Luigi Creatore

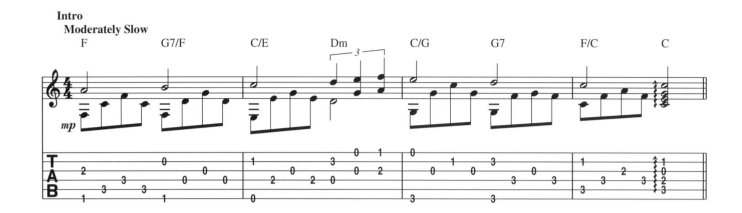

(Everything I Do) I Do It for You

from the Motion Picture ROBIN HOOD: PRINCE OF THIEVES

Words and Music by Bryan Adams, Robert John Lange and Michael Kamen

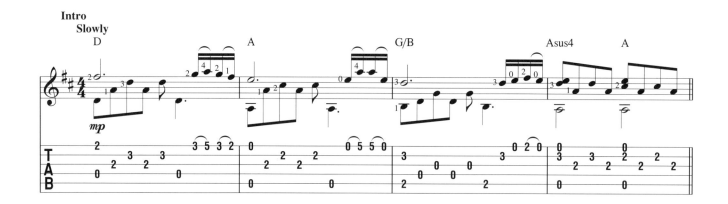

oth - er   could give   more   love.   There's   no ___ way, _____ un - less

you're _ there   all the   time, _____ all the   way, _   yeah. _

Interlude

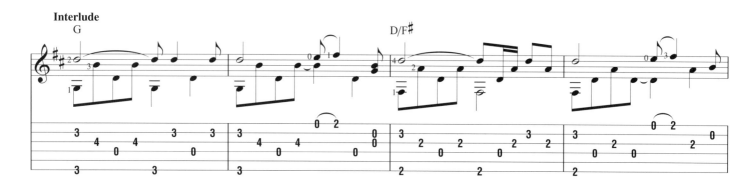

Oh, you can't

Outro-Chorus

Happy Xmas
(War Is Over)
Words and Music by John Lennon and Yoko Ono

Drop D Tuning:
① = E   ④ = D
② = B   ⑤ = A
③ = G   ⑥ = D

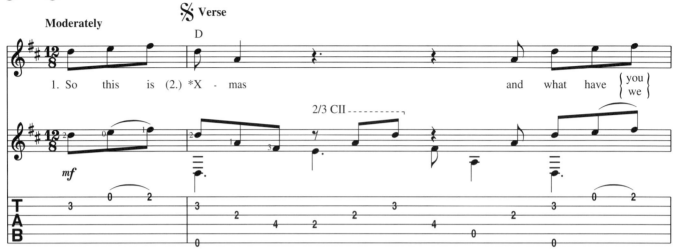

*Sung as "Christmas" throughout.

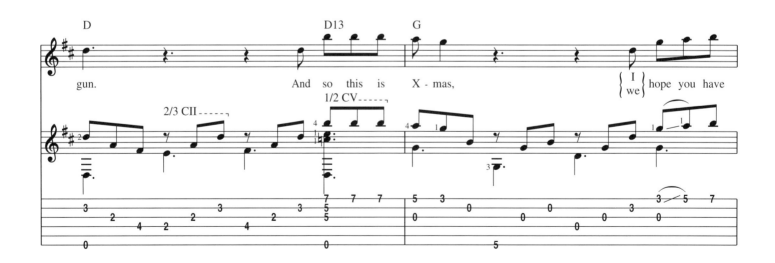

It's a Small World

from "it's a small world" at Disneyland Park and Magic Kingdom Park

Words and Music by Richard M. Sherman and Robert B. Sherman

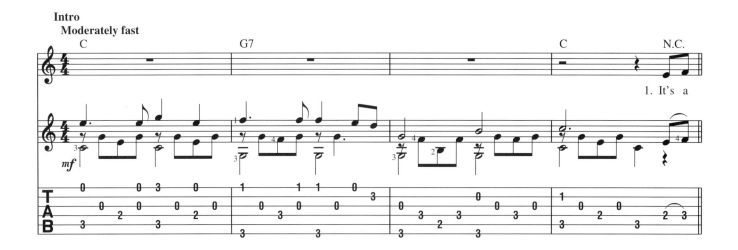

Chorus

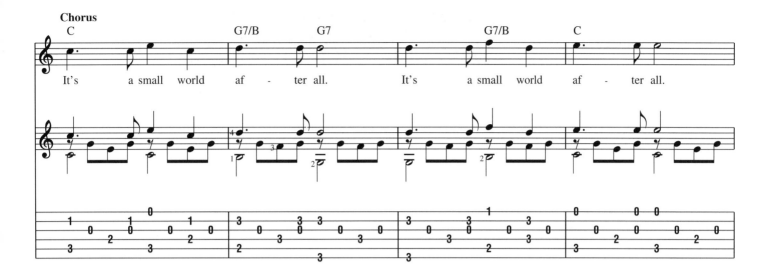

It's a small world af - ter all. It's a small world af - ter all.

D.S. al Coda

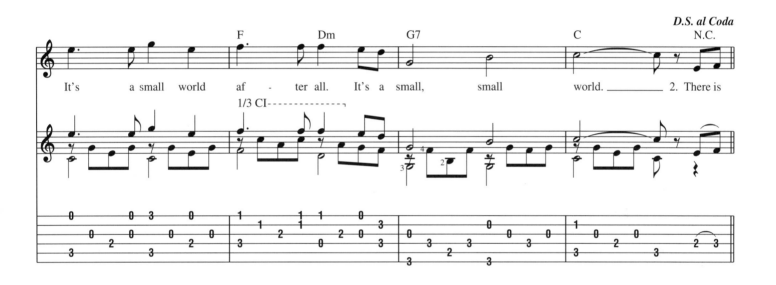

It's a small world af - ter all. It's a small, small world. _____ 2. There is

Coda

Outro

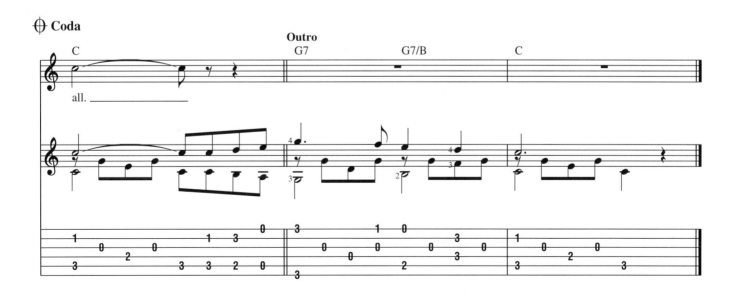

all. _____

This Is the Day
(A Wedding Song)

Words and Music by Scott Wesley Brown

Outro

This is the day, _____ this is the

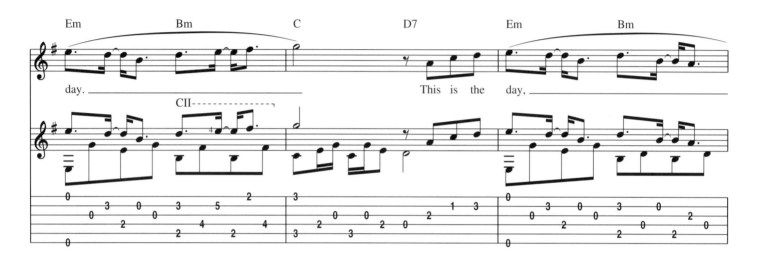

day. _____ This is the day, _____

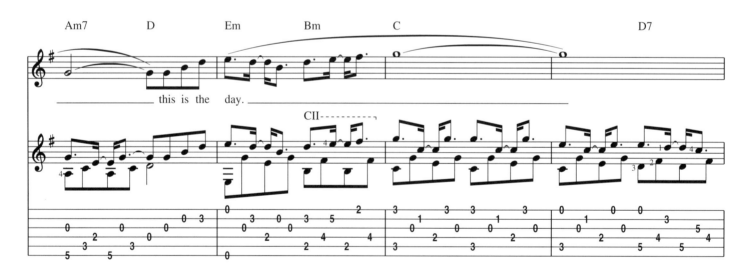

_____ this is the day. _____

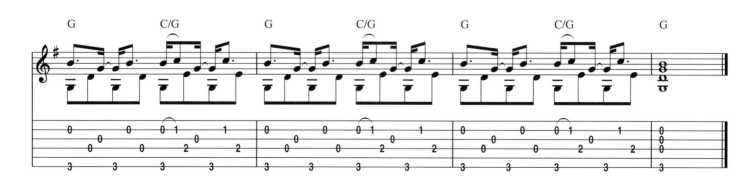

Bark at the Moon

Words and Music by Ozzy Osbourne

Intro

Moderate Rock ♩ = 144

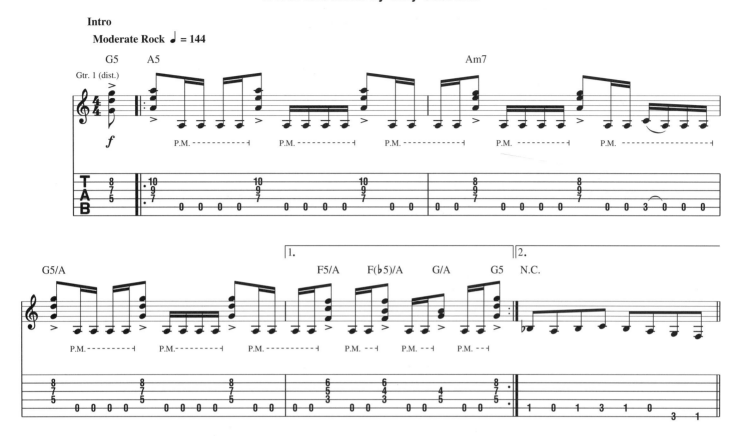

Living After Midnight

Words and Music by Glenn Tipton, Rob Halford and K.K. Downing

Intro

Moderate Rock ♩ = 134

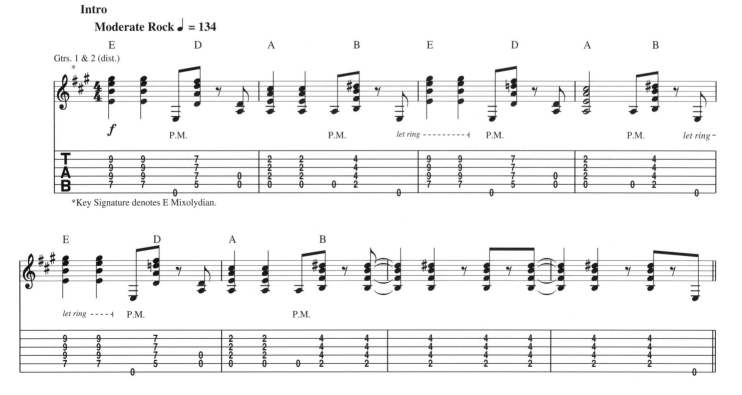

*Key Signature denotes E Mixolydian.

De Do Do Do, De Da Da Da

Music and Lyrics by Sting

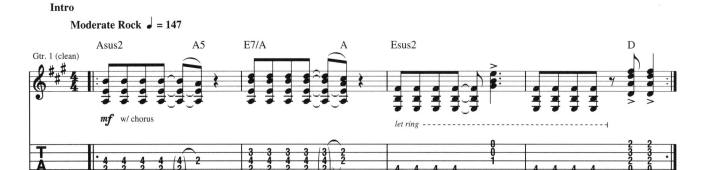

867-5309/ Jenny

Words and Music by Alex Call and James Keller

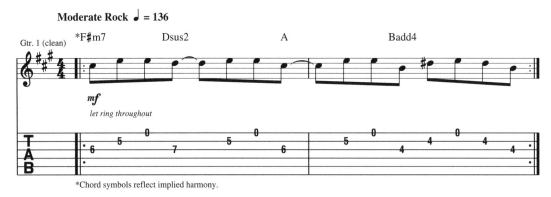

*Chord symbols reflect implied harmony.

Good Morning Little Schoolgirl

Words and Music by Sonny Boy Williamson

I Believe I'll Dust My Broom

Words and Music by Robert Johnson

Open E tuning:
(low to high) E–B–E–G#–B–E

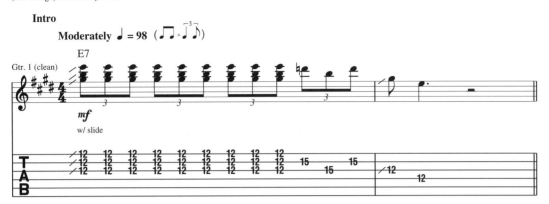

It's Only Love

Words and Music by Bryan Adams and Jim Vallance

Lithium

Words and Music by Kurt Cobain

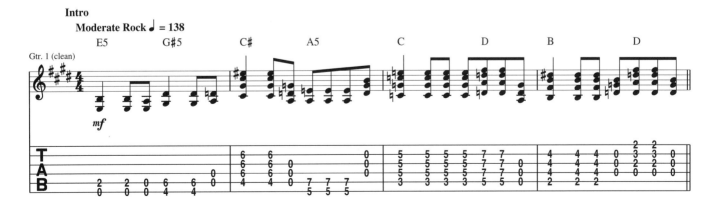

Owner of a Lonely Heart

Words and Music by Trevor Horn, Jon Anderson, Trevor Rabin and Chris Squire

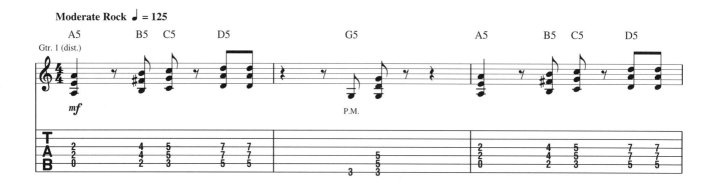

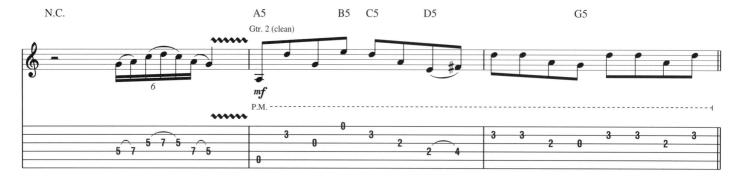

Soul Man

Words and Music by Isaac Hayes and David Porter

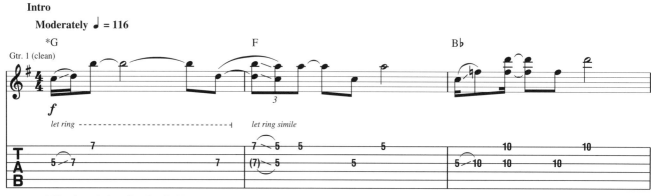

*Chord symbols reflect implied harmony.

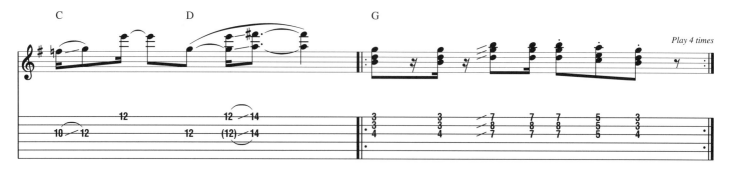

Pink Houses

Words and Music by John Mellencamp

Open G tuning:
(low to high) D–G–D–G–B–D

Intro

Moderately ♩ = 114

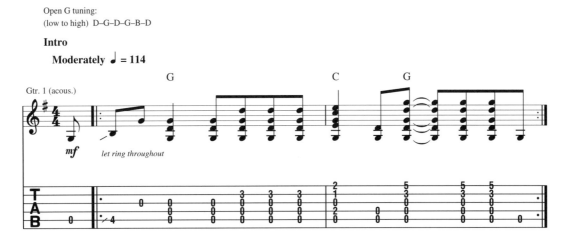

Rock You Like a Hurricane

Words and Music by Herman Rarebell, Klaus Meine and Rudolf Schenker

Intro

Moderate Rock ♩ = 124

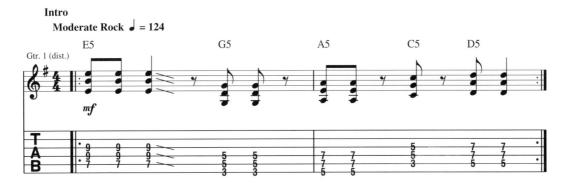

Rollin' Stone
(Catfish Blues)

Written by McKinley Morganfield (Muddy Waters)

Slow Blues ♩ = 88

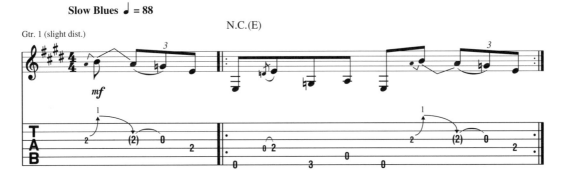

Runnin' Down a Dream

Words and Music by Jeff Lynne, Tom Petty and Mike Campbell

Intro

Bright Rock ♩ = 144

Gtr. 1 (dist.)

N.C.

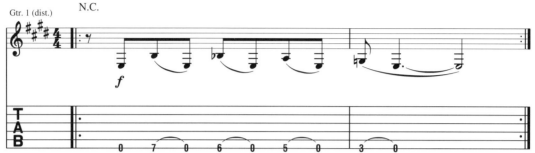

Scuttle Buttin'

Written by Stevie Ray Vaughan

Tune down 1/2 step:
(low to high) Eb–Ab–Db–Gb–Bb–Eb

Moderately fast ♩ = 160

Gtr. 1 (dist.)

N.C.

A Theme

* E7#9

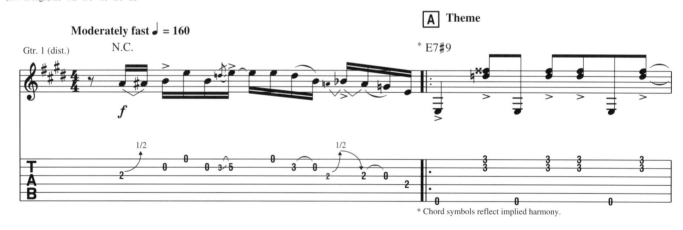

* Chord symbols reflect implied harmony.

N.C.

E7#9

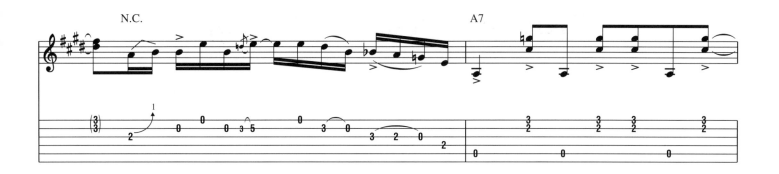

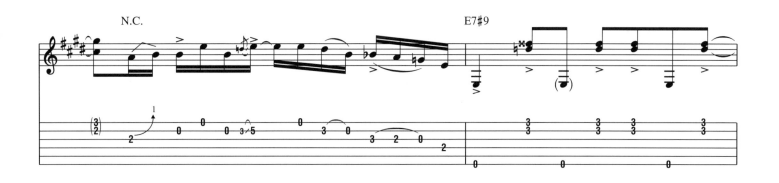

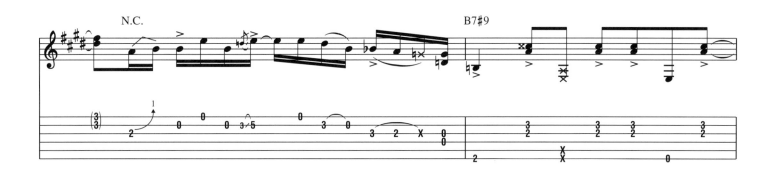

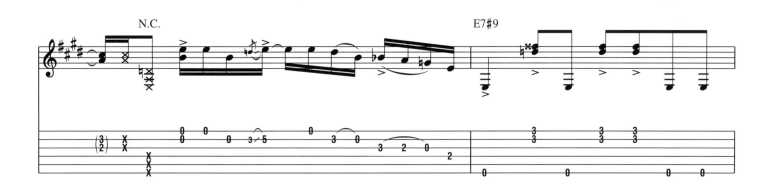

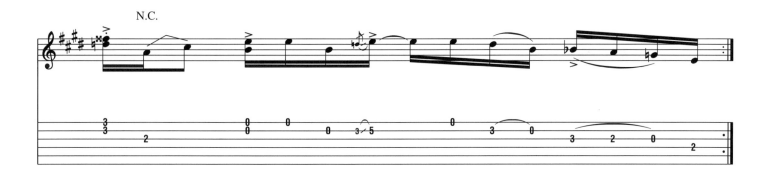

STRUM AND PICK PATTERNS

This chart contains the suggested strum and pick patterns that are referred to by number at the beginning of each song in this book. The symbols ⊓ and ∨ in the strum patterns refer to down and up strokes, respectively. The letters in the pick patterns indicate which right-hand fingers plays which strings.

p = thumb
i = index finger
m = middle finger
a = ring finger

For example; Pick Pattern 2
is played: thumb - index - middle - ring

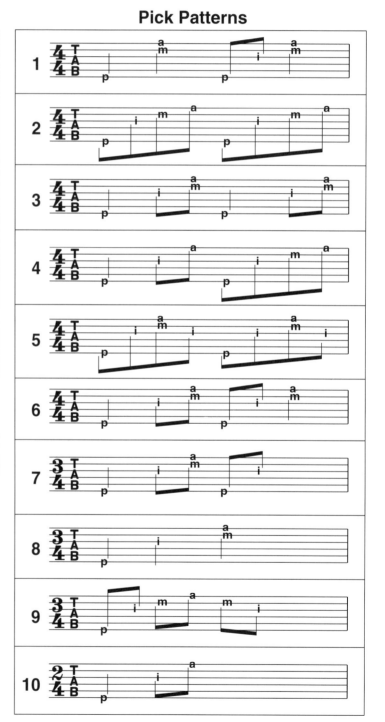

Strum Patterns   ## Pick Patterns

You can use the 3/4 Strum or Pick Patterns in songs written in compound meter (6/8, 9/8, 12/8, etc.).
For example, you can accompany a song in 6/8 by playing the 3/4 pattern twice in each measure.
The 4/4 Strum and Pick Patterns can be used for songs written in cut time (¢) by doubling the note time values in the patterns. Each pattern would therefore last two measures in cut time.

238

Guitar Notation Legend

Guitar Music can be notated three different ways: on a *musical staff*, in *tablature*, and in *rhythm slashes*.

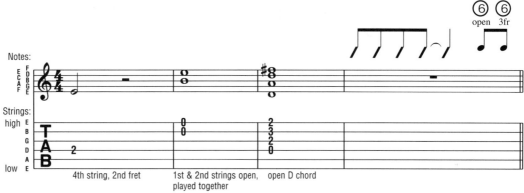

RHYTHM SLASHES are written above the staff. Strum chords in the rhythm indicated. Use the chord diagrams found at the top of the first page of the transcription for the appropriate chord voicings. Round noteheads indicate single notes.

THE MUSICAL STAFF shows pitches and rhythms and is divided by bar lines into measures. Pitches are named after the first seven letters of the alphabet.

TABLATURE graphically represents the guitar fingerboard. Each horizontal line represents a string, and each number represents a fret.

HALF-STEP BEND: Strike the note and bend up 1/2 step.

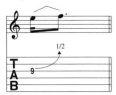

BEND AND RELEASE: Strike the note and bend up as indicated, then release back to the original note. Only the first note is struck.

HAMMER-ON: Strike the first (lower) note with one finger, then sound the higher note (on the same string) with another finger by fretting it without picking.

TRILL: Very rapidly alternate between the notes indicated by continuously hammering on and pulling off.

PICK SCRAPE: The edge of the pick is rubbed down (or up) the string, producing a scratchy sound.

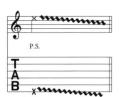

TREMOLO PICKING: The note is picked as rapidly and continuously as possible.

WHOLE-STEP BEND: Strike the note and bend up one step.

PRE-BEND: Bend the note as indicated, then strike it.

PULL-OFF: Place both fingers on the notes to be sounded. Strike the first note and without picking, pull the finger off to sound the second (lower) note.

TAPPING: Hammer ("tap") the fret indicated with the pick-hand index or middle finger and pull off to the note fretted by the fret hand.

MUFFLED STRINGS: A percussive sound is produced by laying the fret hand across the string(s) without depressing, and striking them with the pick hand.

VIBRATO BAR DIVE AND RETURN: The pitch of the note or chord is dropped a specified number of steps (in rhythm) then returned to the original pitch.

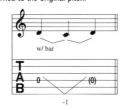

GRACE NOTE BEND: Strike the note and immediately bend up as indicated.

VIBRATO: The string is vibrated by rapidly bending and releasing the note with the fretting hand.

LEGATO SLIDE: Strike the first note and then slide the same fret-hand finger up or down to the second note. The second note is not struck.

NATURAL HARMONIC: Strike the note while the fret-hand lightly touches the string directly over the fret indicated.

PALM MUTING: The note is partially muted by the pick hand lightly touching the string(s) just before the bridge.

VIBRATO BAR SCOOP: Depress the bar just before striking the note, then quickly release the bar.

SLIGHT (MICROTONE) BEND: Strike the note and bend up 1/4 step.

WIDE VIBRATO: The pitch is varied to a greater degree by vibrating with the fretting hand.

SHIFT SLIDE: Same as legato slide, except the second note is struck.

PINCH HARMONIC: The note is fretted normally and a harmonic is produced by adding the edge of the thumb or the tip of the index finger of the pick hand to the normal pick attack.

RAKE: Drag the pick across the strings indicated with a single motion.

VIBRATO BAR DIP: Strike the note and then immediately drop a specified number of steps, then release back to the original pitch.

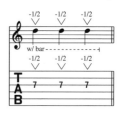

239

GUITAR PLAY-ALONG

INCLUDES TAB

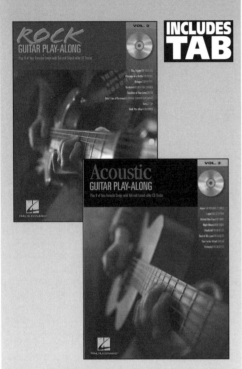

The Guitar Play-Along Series will help you play your favorite songs quickly and easily. Just follow the tab and listen to the CD to hear how the guitar should sound, and then play along using the separate backing tracks. Mac or PC users can also slow down the tempo by using the CD in their computer. The melody and lyrics are also included in the book in case you want to sing, or to simply help you follow along. 8 songs in each book.

VOLUME 1 – ROCK GUITAR

Day Tripper • Message in a Bottle • Refugee • Shattered • Sunshine of Your Love • Takin' Care of Business • Tush • Walk This Way.
00699570 Book/CD Pack $12.95

VOLUME 2 – ACOUSTIC GUITAR

Angie • Behind Blue Eyes • Best of My Love • Blackbird • Dust in the Wind • Layla • Night Moves • Yesterday.
00699569 Book/CD Pack $12.95

VOLUME 3 – HARD ROCK

Crazy Train • Iron Man • Living After Midnight • Rock You like a Hurricane • Round and Round • Smoke on the Water • Sweet Child O' Mine • You Really Got Me.
00699573 Book/CD Pack $14.95

VOLUME 4 – POP/ROCK

Breakdown • Crazy Little Thing Called Love • Hit Me with Your Best Shot • I Want You to Want Me • Lights • R.O.C.K. in the U.S.A. (A Salute to 60's Rock) • Summer of '69 • What I like About You.
_____00699571 Book/CD Pack..........................$12.95

VOLUME 5 – MODERN ROCK

Aerials • Alive • Bother • Chop Suey! • Control • Last Resort • Take a Look Around (Theme from "M:I-2") • Wish You Were Here.
_____00699574 Book/CD Pack..........................$12.95

VOLUME 6 – '90S ROCK

Are You Gonna Go My Way • Come Out and Play • I'll Stick Around • Know Your Enemy • Man in the Box • Outshined • Smells like Teen Spirit • Under the Bridge.
_____00699572 Book/CD Pack..........................$12.95

VOLUME 7 – BLUES GUITAR

All Your Love (I Miss Loving) • Born Under a Bad Sign • Crosscut Saw • I'm Tore Down • Pride and Joy • The Sky Is Crying • Sweet Home Chicago • The Thrill Is Gone.
_____00699575 Book/CD Pack..........................$12.95

VOLUME 8 – ROCK

All Right Now • Black Magic Woman • Get Back • Hey Joe • Layla • Love Me Two Times • Won't Get Fooled Again • You Really Got Me.
_____00699585 Book/CD Pack..........................$12.95

VOLUME 9 – PUNK ROCK

All the Small Things • Fat Lip • Flavor of the Weak • Hash Pipe • I Feel So • Pretty Fly (For a White Guy) • Say It Ain't So • Self Esteem.
_____00699576 Book/CD Pack..........................$12.95

VOLUME 10 – ACOUSTIC

Have You Ever Really Loved a Woman? • Here Comes the Sun • The Magic Bus • Norwegian Wood (This Bird Has Flown) • Space Oddity • Spanish Caravan • Tangled up in Blue • Tears in Heaven.
_____00699586 Book/CD Pack..........................$12.95

VOLUME 11 – EARLY ROCK

Fun, Fun, Fun • Hound Dog • Louie, Louie • No Particular Place to Go • Oh, Pretty Woman • Rock Around the Clock • Under the Boardwalk • Wild Thing.
_____00699579 Book/CD Pack..........................$12.95

VOLUME 12 – POP/ROCK

Every Breath You Take • I Wish It Would Rain • Money for Nothing • Rebel, Rebel • Run to You • Ticket to Ride • Wonderful Tonight • You Give Love a Bad Name.
_____00699587 Book/CD Pack..........................$12.95

VOLUME 13 – FOLK ROCK

Leaving on a Jet Plane • Suite: Judy Blue Eyes • Take Me Home, Country Roads • This Land Is Your Land • Time in a Bottle • Turn! Turn! Turn! (To Everything There Is a Season) • You've Got a Friend • You've Got to Hide Your Love Away.
_____00699581 Book/CD Pack..........................$12.95

VOLUME 14 – BLUES ROCK

Blue on Black • Crossfire • Cross Road Blues (Crossroads) • The House Is Rockin' • La Grange • Move It on Over • Roadhouse Blues • Statesboro Blues.
_____00699582 Book/CD Pack..........................$12.95

VOLUME 15 – R&B

Ain't Too Proud to Beg • Brick House • Get Ready • I Can't Help Myself (Sugar Pie, Honey Bunch) • I Got You (I Feel Good) • I Heard It Through the Grapevine • My Girl • Shining Star.
_____00699583 Book/CD Pack..........................$12.95

VOLUME 16 – JAZZ

All Blues • Black Orpheus • Bluesette • Footprints • Misty • Satin Doll • Stella by Starlight • Tenor Madness.
_____00699584 Book/CD Pack..........................$12.95

VOLUME 17 – COUNTRY

All My Rowdy Friends Are Coming over Tonight • Amie • Boot Scootin' Boogie • Chattahoochee • Folsom Prison Blues • Friends in Low Places • T-R-O-U-B-L-E • Workin' Man Blues.
_____00699588 Book/CD Pack..........................$12.95

VOLUME 18 – ACOUSTIC ROCK

About a Girl • Breaking the Girl • Drive • Iris • More Than Words • Patience • Silent Lucidity • 3 AM.
_____00699577 Book/CD Pack..........................$12.95

VOLUME 19 – SOUL

Get up (I Feel like Being) a Sex Machine • Green Onions • In the Midnight Hour • Knock on Wood • Mustang Sally • (Sittin' On) the Dock of the Bay • Soul Man • Walkin' the Dog.
_____00699578 Book/CD Pack..........................$12.95

VOLUME 20 – ROCKABILLY

Blue Suede Shoes • Bluejean Bop • Hello Mary Lou • Little Sister • Mystery Train • Rock This Town • Stray Cat Strut • That'll Be the Day.
_____00699580 Book/CD Pack..........................$12.95

Prices, contents, and availability subject to change without notice.

FOR MORE INFORMATION, SEE YOUR LOCAL MUSIC DEALER, OR WRITE TO:

HAL•LEONARD
CORPORATION
7777 W. BLUEMOUND RD. P.O. BOX 13819 MILWAUKEE, WI 53213

Visit Hal Leonard online at www.halleonard.com